THE PURSUIT OF WISDOM

THE PURSUIT OF WISDOM

125 PRAYERS
FROM TIMELESS VOICES

edited by
THOMAS BECKNELL
MARY ELLEN ASHCROFT

judson press
VALLEY FORGE

The Pursuit of Wisdom: 125 Prayers from Timeless Voices

The authors have made every effort to trace the ownership of all quotes. We regret any error made. In the event of a question arising from the use of a quote, please notify the publisher promptly, and we will be pleased to make the necessary correction in future printings and editions of this book.

Bible quotations in this volume are from the New Revised Standard Version, copyright © 1989 by the Division of Christian Education of the National Council of the Churches of Christ in the United States of America. Used by permission. All rights reserved.

Library of Congress Cataloging-in-Publication Data

The pursuit of wisdom : 125 prayers from timeless voices / [edited by] Thomas Becknell, Mary Ellen Ashcroft.
    p. cm.
Includes index.
ISBN 0-8170-1427-6 (pbk. : alk. paper)
1. Prayers. I. Becknell, Thomas. II. Ashcroft, Mary Ellen, 1952–.

BV245 .P95 2002
242'.8--dc21

                                   2001050412

Printed in the U.S.A.

09 08 07 06 05 04 03 02

10 9 8 7 6 5 4 3 2 1

CONTENTS

ACKNOWLEDGMENTS

W e are grateful to all those who, in their pursuit of wisdom and understanding, set down their prayers in writing. We are thankful, too, for our students, friends, and colleagues at Bethel College who helped to make this book possible. Special thanks to Donna LeGrand, Richard Peterson, Linde Getahun, Thomas Johnson, and Deb Harless for their assistance.

Grateful acknowledgment is made to the following for permission to reprint previously published material.

Excerpt by Anna of Freiburg, translated from the *Ausbund* by Linde Getahun and Thomas Johnson. Used by permission.

Excerpt taken from *Prayer in a Troubled World* by George Appleton. Copyright © Darton, Longman and Todd, Ltd. (London). Used by permission of the publishers.

INTRODUCTION

In a world of talk-show celebrities, instant credit, and twenty-minute solutions to sitcom dilemmas, who wants wisdom? We can hardly relate to Solomon, who chose wisdom when God offered him whatever he wanted—we would have taken wealth. Or to the apostle Paul, who prayed that the church would be filled with the knowledge of God—we would have chosen that our church be filled with people who put hefty checks in the offering plate. We've forgotten that to the Hebrew mind wisdom was eminently practical, helping the wise to distinguish between right and wrong, to follow God's path. We have more often pulled our images of wisdom from Greek thought, where we encounter an otherworldly sage contemplating the mysteries or a clever debater arguing minuscule points with great verbal agility.

This doesn't appeal to us, so wisdom has sunk to the bottom of our wish list.

Despite wisdom's low ratings, we need it desperately. The beginning of wisdom is recognition of our need for God and for growth—a need that has governed the men and women who are our parents in the faith. They set an example for us by pursuing wisdom as if it were a matter of life and death.

The men and women whose prayers are represented in this book, some without formal education, some with immense depths of learning, have all pursued wisdom. And all of them are known for their praying. Missionary or mystic, teacher or activist, scientist or poet, they teach us here, not through a demonstration of their intellect, but through the example of their prayers. From them we learn the secret of surrounding the journey toward wisdom with prayer.

Most of us know that learning happens in a variety of settings—from volunteer work in a ghetto, to an encounter with a new culture thousands of miles from home, to an Outward Bound ropes course, to the quiet corner of a bedroom where we open a book, to the community orchestra where we learn to blend our harmonies with those of other amateur musicians. And learning happens in more formal settings—in schools and universities, book discussion groups, Sunday school classes, and Bible studies. Growth often catches us in one of these "classrooms."

When we care deeply about anything in our lives—our families, our vocations, our countries—we pray about them. And so it should be with our pursuit of wisdom. We bring ourselves, individually or corporately, to God, asking that our learning and growth may be a collaboration with the Source of all wisdom. And as we move toward greater understanding, we need prayer—when we struggle with failure (or success), when we encounter feelings of inadequacy and uncertainty, when we long for clarity and focus. We are compelled to pray.

But sometimes words fail us. "Your thoughts don't have words every day," wrote the poet Emily Dickinson. When we are committing our growth to God, as our minds are being stretched or when our perspective of the world or of ourselves is being shifted, we may feel driven to pray but struggle to find the right words.

The Pursuit of Wisdom grew out of our own practical need to find words that would articulate for us, in prayer, the complex thoughts and emotions that seem to accompany almost any experience of learning. What we have found from using these prayers in our own classrooms, with other teachers, and in our personal prayer lives is that these are eminently "prayable" prayers—clear, useful, heart-driven expressions of men and women who have prayed well.

These are prayers to encourage you in your pursuit of growth and understanding. The sequence of six chapters is designed to complement the natural process of learning, beginning with prayers of praise and thanksgiving and concluding with prayers for a vision of the world as love would make. To those unaccustomed to using written prayers, these expressions can be liberating. Freed from the distraction of trying to compose our thoughts, we can use these words to concentrate on the act of prayer itself—an act that requires more listening than speaking. We hope that, in using them, you'll find prayer becoming a natural part of the process of learning, whether in the course of formal learning or in the lifelong experience of learning outside the classroom.

CHAPTER 1

PRAYERS TO THE SOURCE
OF ALL WISDOM

The story of Solomon's wisdom and how he got it is a familiar one to anyone who has attended Sunday school. Pleased that the new king, Solomon, did not ask for wealth, honor, long life, or victory over his enemies, God granted his request for wisdom and understanding. And in addition to unparalleled wisdom, God gave Solomon unsurpassed wealth and prestige (1 Kings 3:3-14).

The Old and New Testaments persistently urge us to seek wisdom above wealth. Indeed, wisdom is one of the few commodities we are specifically instructed to ask for: "If any of you is lacking in wisdom," writes James, "ask God, who gives to all generously and ungrudgingly" (James 1:5).

The prayers in this first chapter acknowledge God as the source of all wisdom. Many of these are ancient prayers—from Thomas Aquinas, Catherine of Siena, Clement of Alexandria, the apostle Paul, and others. Perhaps those early Christians recognized, more readily than modern Christians do, the limits of human wisdom and understanding. "Though I do not know myself," prayed Hilary, a fourth-century Christian, "yet I perceive so much that I marvel at thee the more because I am ignorant of myself." We praise the source of faith and learning, not only because God expects our adoration, but also because it preserves us from intellectual arrogance. Or as Thomas Troeger puts it, praise of God protects us from "the blunder / of believing that our thought / has displaced the grounds for wonder / which the ancient prophets taught."

These prayers to the source of all wisdom provide an essential starting point for those who seek growth and understanding. Wisdom, like prayer itself, begins with God. "The fear of the Lord is the beginning of wisdom" (Proverbs 9:10).

give us wisdom

O Gracious and holy Father,
   Give us wisdom to perceive thee,
      intelligence to understand thee,
      diligence to seek thee,
      patience to wait for thee,
      eyes to behold thee,
      a heart to meditate upon thee,
      and a life to proclaim thee;
   through the power of the Spirit
      of Jesus Christ our Lord.

Born in Nursia in north-central Italy, Benedict (480–547) is regarded as the founder of Western monasticism. While living as a monk at the monastery of Monte Cassino, Benedict wrote the famous "Rule of Benedict," which emphasizes work and prayer. This rule continues to serve as a guide for monastic life today.

the fountain of all wisdom

I implore you, good Jesus, that as in your mercy you have given me to drink in with delight the words of your knowledge, so of your loving kindness you will also grant me one day to come to you, the fountain of all wisdom, and to stand for ever before your face. Amen.

A historian and monk of the early Middle Ages, Bede (673– 735) became known as the "venerable" Bede because of his holy life. His book, *Ecclesiastical History of the English People*, provided a carefully documented record of the development of Christianity in Anglo-Saxon England. This prayer appears above his grave in Durham Cathedral.

for those who teach
and those who learn

❧ THE BOOK OF COMMON PRAYER ❧

Almighty God, the fountain of all wisdom: Enlighten by your Holy Spirit those who teach and those who learn, that, rejoicing in the knowledge of your truth, they may worship you and serve you from generation to generation; through Jesus Christ our Lord, who lives and reigns with you and the Holy Spirit, one God, for ever and ever. Amen.

The Book of Common Prayer—first composed by Thomas Cranmer, archbishop of Canterbury, in 1549—continues to serve as a guide to worship within the Anglican Communion worldwide, including the Episcopal Church.

teach me to know you here on earth

~ ELISABETH ELLIOT ~

Lord, you have said, I am the Way—not that we
    shall never be confused.
You have said, I am the Truth—not that we shall
    have all the answers.
And, I am the Life—not that we shall never die.
Teach me to know you here on earth—
    in its tangled maze of pathways, to know you
    as the Way;
    in its unanswerable mysteries, to know you
    as the Truth;
    in the face of suffering and death, to know you
    as the Life.
Thank you, Lord, for not offering us a method,
    saying, This is the Way.
Thank you for not granting us a set of invariable
    propositions, saying, This is the Truth.
Thank you for not delivering us from being human,
    saying, This is the Life.
Thank you, Lord, for saying instead, I am, and for
    giving us yourself.

Born in Brussels, Belgium, to missionary parents, Elisabeth
Elliot Gren was married to Jim Elliot, one of five American missionaries martyred by Auca Indians in Ecuador in 1956. She told
that story in her book *Through Gates of Splendor*. Elisabeth Elliot
Gren is the author of a number of other books as well.

to learn

⌒ ERASMUS ⌒

Hear our prayers, O Lord Jesus, the everlasting Wisdom of the Father; who givest unto us, in the days of our youth, aptness to learn: Add, we pray thee, the furtherance of thy grace, so to learn knowledge and the liberal sciences that, by their help, we may attain to the fuller knowing of thee, whom to know is the height of blessedness; and by the example of thy boyhood, may duly increase in age, wisdom, and favour with God and man.

Desiderius Erasmus of Rotterdam (1466–1536) was perhaps the most important and influential Christian humanist of the northern Renaissance. He was called the "prince of the humanists," and his concern for Christian piety and his commitment to education and learning have made him an important role model for educated Christians.

the wisdom and knowledge of god

O the depth of the riches both of the wisdom and knowledge of God! How unsearchable are his judgments, and his ways past finding out! For who hath known the mind of the Lord? Or who hath been his counselor? Or who hath first given to him, and it shall be recompensed unto him again? For of him, and through him, and to him, are all things: to whom be glory for ever. Amen.

Saul of Tarsus was converted to Christianity on the road to Damascus after persecuting the church. He thereafter became an apostle, planting churches and teaching the new believers in what are now Turkey and Greece. This prayer is taken from his letter to the largely Gentile church in Rome, written around A.D. 57.

great god of all wisdom

⌒ JANE PARKER HUBER ⌒

Great God of all wisdom, of science and art,
O grant us the wisdom that comes from the heart.
Technology, learning, philosophy, youth—
All leave us still yearning for your word of truth.

Where people are starving, where wars devastate,
A future we're carving of anguish and hate.
God, turn us around and invade all our lives
Till justice is found and your righteousness thrives.

Call us to a new day of promise and trust
That outlines a new way of life that is just.
Call us to build bridges, deep chasms to clear,
Mark trails over ridges of bias and fear.

Creator of visions as well as of stars,
O mend our divisions and heal all our scars.
You reign over history, both present and past,
Most challenging mystery from first to the last.

Born in 1926 in Tsinan, China, Jane Parker Huber was educated at Northfield School for Girls, Wellesley College, and Hanover College. She is well known in Presbyterian circles for her work with the Presbyterian Women, for her many hymns, and for her dedication to social justice and peacemaking.

o creator,
shed the light of your wisdom

❦ ST. THOMAS AQUINAS ❧

O Creator of the universe, who has set the stars in the heavens and causes the sun to rise and set, shed the light of your wisdom into the darkness of my mind. Fill my thoughts with the loving knowledge of you, that I may bring your light to others. Just as you can make even babies speak your truth, instruct my tongue and guide my pen to convey the wonderful glory of the gospel. Make my intellect sharp, my memory clear, and my words eloquent, so that I may faithfully interpret the mysteries which you have revealed.

Thomas Aquinas (1225–74), born at the family castle of Roccasecca (between Rome and Naples), was related to the emperor and king of France and was destined by his parents to be abbot of Monte Cassino, where he went to school. Because he was determined to join a Dominican order, his family imprisoned him for fifteen months. When he joined the order, he studied, taught, and wrote in several cities. He is best known for his *Summa Theologica*, through which he explored issues of reason and faith.

enlighten the darkness of my heart

⌒ FRANCIS OF ASSISI ⌒

O most high, glorious God, enlighten the darkness
of my heart and give me
    a right faith,
       a certain hope
           and a perfect love, understanding
    and knowledge,
O Lord,
    that I may carry out your holy and true command.
Amen.

Many legends have grown up around the life of Francis of
Assisi (1182–1226). Converted to Christianity at age twenty-three,
he lived a life of deliberate poverty. In 1208 he set out on foot
to preach the gospel. Others, inspired by his gentleness and his
service to the poor, formed a religious order, the Franciscans.

this complex tapestry

~ CLIFFORD SWARTZ ~

All things worship thee,
Revealing by their form and actions
The patterns of creation.
This complex tapestry is proper subject
For analysis and praise.
By such study, humans worship their creator,
And fulfill their proper role
Which is the understanding of this world.
The songs of great composers or the whales
Are meaningless without the tutored ear.
The sunsets and cathedrals are diminished
When we are blind to intricate details.
Worship in this highest form must be creative.

But we can praise thee in a simpler way.
The soaring gull caresses rising air,
The dolphins leap in play, and lovers are enraptured.
When creatures revel in the joy of life
They also worship their creator.
Perhaps the bursting gladness of this world
Can balance out the cries of anguish.

If we believe that this is so,
And that there is a purpose

In the universal scheme
And in our individual lives,
We also worship thee.

Clifford Swartz is professor of physics at the University of New York, Stony Brook, and author of a number of physics textbooks. He first began writing prayers in the choir loft at his church.

a prayer of wonder

∽ RICHARD J. FOSTER ∾

I glory in your handiwork, O God:
   towering mountains and deep valleys,
   dense forests and expansive deserts,
   fathomless depths of blue below and immeasurable
   heights of blue above.

When I peer into the universe of the telescope and
the universe of the microscope I stand in awe at:
   the complexity and the simplicity,
   the order and the chaos,
   and the infinite variety of colors everywhere.

When I watch the little creatures that creep upon the
earth I marvel at:
   such purpose,
      such direction,
         such design;
   and yet
      such freedom,
         such openness,
            such creativity.

O Lord God, Creator of the hummingbird and the Milky
Way, I am lost in wonder at your originality. Amen.

Born in New Mexico and author of several books, including
Prayer: Finding the Heart's True Home and *Celebration of Discipline*,
Richard Foster is an ordained minister in the Society of Friends.

prayer from nicaragua

ᡣ— CARLOS MEJÍA GODOY —ᡣ

Firmly I believe, Lord,
that your prodigious mind
created this whole earth.
To your artist's hand
beauty owed its birth:
the stars and the moon,
the cottages, the lakes,
little boats bobbing
down river to the sea,
vast coffee plantations,
white cotton fields
and the forests felled
by the criminal axe. . . .

In you I believe,
maker of thought and music,
maker of the wind,
maker of peace and love.

Carlos Mejía Godoy is a well-known poet, musician, and actor in his native Nicaragua, and he is the composer of some of Nicaragua's most popular songs. His mass, the *Misa Campesina*, in which this prayer appears, is regarded as one of the greatest expressions of Nicaraguan culture.

to walk in your power

✑ ANNA OF FREIBURG ✑

My eternal Lord and Father,
Show wisdom and learning
To this your humble child,
That I might attend to your ways
For such is my yearning.

To walk in your power facing death,
Through sadness, pain, fear, and need,
In all of this sustain me
That I might never be estranged
From your love, O God.

Many travel on this road,
Bearing the cup of sorrow,
And also many false teachings,
That try to lead us astray
From Christ our Lord.

In the power of God I do not doubt
So truthful is his judgment;
He will not abandon
Those who stand firm in faith
And remain on the path.

In 1529, while yet a teenager, Anna of Freiburg was drowned
and then burned for her Anabaptist faith. This prayer comes from
a much longer hymn attributed to her in the *Ausbund*, the collection of the earliest hymns of the Swiss Anabaptists.

prayer for wisdom

TRADITIONAL NATIVE AMERICAN PRAYER

O Great Spirit
whose voice I hear in the winds,
and whose breath gives life to all the world,
hear me! I am small and weak, I need your strength
and wisdom.

Let me walk in beauty, and make my eyes ever behold
the red and purple sunset.

Make my hands respect the things you have made
and my ears sharp to hear your voice.

Make me wise so that I may understand the things you
have taught my people.

Let me learn the lessons you have hidden in every leaf
and rock.

I seek strength, not to be greater than my brother,
but to fight my greatest enemy—myself.

Make me always ready to come to you with clean hands
and straight eyes.

So when life fades, as the fading sunset,
my spirit may come to you without shame.

Native American spirituality is generally characterized by a
belief that everything in creation is sacred and that all of life—
human and nonhuman—is interrelated.

17

praise the source
of faith and learning

∽ THOMAS H. TROEGER ∽

Praise the source of faith and learning
who has sparked and stoked the mind
with a passion for discerning
how the world has been designed.
Let the sense of wonder flowing
from the wonders we survey
keep our faith forever growing
and renew our need to pray:

God of wisdom, we acknowledge
that our science and our art
and the breadth of human knowledge
only partial truth impart.
Far beyond our calculation
lies a depth we cannot sound
where your purpose for creation
and the pulse of life are found.

May our faith redeem the blunder
of believing that our thought
has displaced the grounds for wonder
which the ancient prophets taught.
May our learning curb the error
which unthinking faith can breed
lest we justify some terror
with an antiquated creed.

As two currents in a river
fight each other's undertow
till converging they deliver
one coherent steady flow,
blend, O God, our faith and learning
till they carve a single course,
while they join as one returning
praise and thanks to you their source.

A Presbyterian minister and professor at the Iliff School of
Theology, Thomas H. Troeger is the author of such books as *Are
You Saved? Answers to the Awkward Question* (1979), *Ten
Strategies for Preaching in a Multimedia Culture* (1996), and
Preaching While the Church Is under Construction (1999).

pied beauty

∽ GERARD MANLEY HOPKINS ∼

Glory be to God for dappled things—
     For skies of couple-colour as a brinded cow;
          For rose-moles all in stipple upon trout that swim;
Fresh-firecoal chestnut-falls; finches' wings;
     Landscapes plotted and pieced—
     fold, fallow, and plough;
          And all trades, their gear and tackle and trim.

All things counter, original, spare, strange;
     Whatever is fickle, freckled (who knows how?)
          With swift, slow; sweet, sour; adazzle, dim;
He fathers-forth whose beauty is past change:
                    Praise him.

Born near London, Gerard Manley Hopkins (1844–89) attended Oxford and originally planned to become a painter. But when he joined the Catholic Church at age twenty-two, he changed his mind and decided to become a Jesuit. At age forty, he took a post as professor of classics at University College in Dublin, but he died of typhoid a few years later. His poetry was not collected and published until 1918.

o educator, father

∽ CLEMENT OF ALEXANDRIA ∽

O Educator, be gracious to thy children, O Educator, Father, guide of Israel, Son and Father, both one, Lord. Give to us, who follow thy command, to fulfill the likeness of thy image, and to see, according to our strength, the God who is both a good God and a Judge who is not harsh. Do thou thyself bestow all things on us who dwell in thy peace, who have been placed in thy city, who sail the sea of sin unruffled, that we may be made tranquil and supported by the Holy Spirit, the unutterable Wisdom, by night and day, unto the perfect day, to sing eternal thanksgiving to the one only Father and Son, Son and Father, Educator and Teacher with the Holy Spirit. All things are for the One, in whom are all things, through whom eternity is, of whom all men are members, to whom is glory, and the ages, whose are all things in their goodness; all things, in their beauty; all things, in their wisdom; all things, in their justice. To him be glory now and forever. Amen.

Clement of Alexandria (c.150–215), probably an Athenian by birth, was a theologian. Forced by persecution to leave his homeland in 202, he tried to bring the best of Greek philosophy to bear on Christian theology. He taught that Christ, the Logos, was both an interpreter of God to humanity and the source of all human reason. Clement was martyred around 215.

you, eternal truth

∽ CATHERINE OF SIENA ∽

You, O Eternal Trinity, are a deep sea, into which the more I enter, the more I find, and the more I find, the more I seek. The soul cannot be satisfied in your abyss, for she continually hungers after you, the Eternal Trinity, desiring to see you with the light of your light.

As the hart desires the springs of living water, so my soul desires to leave the prison of this dark body and see you in truth.

O abyss, O Eternal Godhead, O sea profound, what more could you give me than yourself? You are the fire that ever burns without being consumed; you consume in your heat all the soul's self-love; you are the fire which takes away cold; with your light you illuminate me so that I may know all your truth. Clothe me, clothe me with yourself, Eternal Truth, so that I may run this mortal life with true obedience, and with light of your most holy faith.

As a young woman, Catherine Benincasa of Siena (1347–80) once cut off her hair to discourage suitors. In time she became a Dominican nun, known for her service to the poor and sick and for her conversion of sinners. She eventually became a highly sought-after spiritual authority. She never learned to write, but she dictated her letters and a book.

with christ in the school of prayer

∽ ANDREW MURRAY ∽

O my blessed Lord Jesus, teach me to understand Your lesson, that it is the indwelling Spirit, streaming from You, uniting to You, who is the Spirit of prayer. Teach me what it is as an empty, wholly consecrated vessel, to yield myself to His being my life. Teach me to honor and trust Him, as a living person, to lead my life and my prayer. Teach me especially in prayer to wait in holy silence, and give Him place to breathe within me His unutterable intercession. And teach me that through Him it is possible to pray without ceasing, and to pray without failing, because He makes me partaker of the never-ceasing and never-failing intercession in which You, the Son, appear before the Father.

Born in South Africa in 1828, Andrew Murray studied theology in Europe. He served in a number of Dutch Reformed Churches in the Orange Free State and the Cape Colony. He is best remembered for his many devotional books, such as *Like Christ, With Christ in the School of Prayer,* and *Holy in Christ*.

CHAPTER 2

PRAYERS TO PREPARE
THE HEART AND MIND

Often the most difficult part of a learning experience is the preparation. Sometimes we simply cannot find the time to open a book, to prepare a lesson, or even to think; the press of other duties or the call of other voices keep us from it. Sometimes we struggle with discouragement or weariness or lack of confidence. And sometimes the terror of the blank page or the tediousness of the research or the complexity of a problem overwhelms us.

These prayers show us how to ask for God's help in facing the challenges of learning. They are remarkably clear, practical expressions that can assist us in sorting through the muddled thoughts and emotions we may feel at such times.

Some of these prayers will encourage us to name specifically the barriers and distractions we confront.

Mechthild of Magdeburg prays simply, "Please, wake me up." W. E. B. Du Bois sees the barrier of procrastination and prays for help in learning that "today. . . our best studying can be done and not some future day or future year." Sarah Klos is concerned about the worry and indifference and frenzy in her classroom. Theodore Roethke, in his "Prayer before Study," asks for deliverance from the self-centeredness that he finds so constricting. And a "Prayer from Kenya" confesses that our own cowardice, laziness, and arrogance get in the way of understanding.

Certain prayers also help us to appreciate the complexity of the learning process and to ask for God's guidance and direction. "Broaden our ideas," prays Origen, and some of these prayers will indeed broaden our ideas. Susanna Wesley, for example, explains that all of her intellectual, philosophical, and rhetorical skills will mean nothing to her if she does not also acquire a heart-driven, *experiential* knowledge of God. John Calvin reminds us that the mind, the memory, the heart, and the understanding must all be integrated with God's help. Believing, then, that the spiritual life and the intellectual life are thoroughly integrated, Herbert Brokering can pray, "Come to me in my mind, Jesus," and Oswald Chambers can ask, "Lord, interpret Yourself to me."

Above all, we learn to be direct and straightforward in our requests for God's guidance. These individuals do not beat around the bush in their prayers; they say exactly what they need: "invigorate my studies, and direct my inquiries"; "strengthen my memory"; "teach me to listen"; "bestow upon us the meaning of words"; "help me really to get into things." Praying such prayers will prepare our hearts and enable us to take our minds off our insecurities and other outside distractions, to remain attentive and receptive, and to focus confidently upon the task before us.

prayer from kenya

∽ AUTHOR UNKNOWN ∽

From the cowardice that dare not face new truth
From the laziness that is contented with half-truth
From the arrogance that thinks it knows all truth,
Good Lord, deliver me.

The church in Africa is said to be the fastest-growing church in the world. This prayer, although anonymous, expresses some of the clear-sighted courage and perspective of many African Christians.

prayers before study

∽ SAMUEL JOHNSON ∾

Almighty God, our heavenly Father, without whose help labor is useless, without whose light search is vain, invigorate my studies, and direct my inquiries, that I may, by due diligence and right discernment, establish myself and others in your holy faith. Take not, O Lord, your Holy Spirit from me; let not evil thoughts have dominion in my mind. Let me not linger in ignorance, but enlighten and support me, for the sake of Jesus Christ our Lord. Amen.

Almighty God, the Giver of Wisdom, without whose help resolutions are vain, without whose blessing study is ineffectual, enable me, if it be thy will, to attain such knowledge as may qualify me to direct the doubtful, and instruct the ignorant, to prevent wrongs, and terminate contentions; and grant that I may use that knowledge which I shall attain, to your glory and my own salvation, for Jesus Christ's sake. Amen.

Remembered as an author, lexicographer, and conversationalist, Samuel Johnson (1709–84) was also known in his own day for his high-church piety as a member of the Church of England. He was generous with the pen and faithful in his religious duties.

christ our teacher

∽ JANET MORLEY ∾

Christ our teacher,
you reach into our lives
not through instruction, but story.
Open our hearts to be attentive;
that seeing, we may perceive,
and hearing, we may understand,
and understanding, may act upon your word,
in your name. Amen.

Janet Morley is adult education adviser for the relief organization Christian Aid. She was active in the Movement for the Ordination of Women in the Anglican Church in the United Kingdom. She is also a contributor to, and coeditor of, the worship anthology *Celebrating Women*.

teach us, o god, that now is the time

∽ W. E. B. DU BOIS ∽

Teach us, O God, that now is the accepted time—not tomorrow, not some more convenient season. It is *today* that our best studying can be done and not some future day or future year. It is *today* that we fit ourselves for the greater usefulness of tomorrow. *Today* is the seed time, *now* are the hours of work and tomorrow comes the harvest and the play-time. May we learn in youth, when the evil days come not, that the man who plays and then works, rests and then studies, fails and then rushes, is not simply reversing nature, he is missing opportunities and losing the training and preparation which makes work and study and endeavor the touchstone of success.

W. E. B. Du Bois (1868–1963), an African American sociologist best known for his book *The Souls of Black Folk* (1903), opposed the positions of racial compromise and acceptance espoused by Booker T. Washington. The work of Du Bois significantly influenced the thinking of such major twentieth-century writers as Ralph Ellison, Malcolm X, and Toni Morrison.

lord, interpret yourself to me

∂— OSWALD CHAMBERS —∂

O Lord, this morning disperse every mist, and shine clear and strong and invigoratingly. Forgive my tardiness, it takes me so long to awaken to some things. Lord God Omniscient, give me wisdom this day to worship and work aright and be well-pleasing to you. Lord, interpret Yourself to me more and more in fullness and beauty.

Oswald Chambers (1874–1917) was born in Aberdeen, Scotland. He was principal of the Bible Training School at Clapham, England, and superintendent of the YMCA camp at Zeitoun, Egypt. His best-known book is *My Utmost for His Highest*, a devotional classic.

morning prayer

~ ELAINE SOMMERS RICH ~

Lord, You are the water of life.
As this day begins, I am an empty pitcher before You.
Fill me, O Lord.

You are the light of the world.
As this day begins, I am an unlit candle.
Your light can never shine through me to others unless
You shine in my heart.
You are the true light that lights every one
That comes into the world.
Light me, O Lord.

You are the true vine.
Unless I dwell in You this day,
I can bring forth no fruit.
My leaves turn brown, shrivel, blow away and I die.
Let Your life always flow into me, Your branch,
        O Lord.

Elaine Sommers Rich is a freelance writer and teacher living in Bluffton, Ohio. She and her husband, Dr. Ronald Rich, spent more than ten years at the International Christian University in Tokyo. She is a longtime columnist for the *Mennonite Weekly Review* and is the author of *Prayers for Everyday* and other books.

please, wake me up

⌁ MECHTHILD OF MAGDEBURG ⌁

O sweet and loving God,
When I stay asleep too long,
Oblivious to all your many blessings,
Then, please, wake me up,
And sing to me your joyful song.
It is a song without noise or notes.
It is a song of love beyond words,
Of faith beyond the power of human telling.
I can hear it in my soul,
When you awaken me to your presence.

Unhappy with the lack of humility in her noble family in
Saxony, Mechthild of Magdeburg (c.1210–80) fled to Magdeburg
to become a Beguine, that is, a lay sister who lived in a religious
community not bound by vows. She led a life of penance and
prayer, and her visions of God, published as *The Light of
Godhead*, deeply influenced German medieval spirituality.

put your word in my mind

∾— JAKOB BÖHME —∾

Rule over me this day, O God, leading me on the path of righteousness. Put your Word in my mind and your Truth in my heart, that this day I neither think nor feel anything except what is good and honest. Protect me from all lies and falsehood, helping me to discern deception wherever I meet it. Let my eyes always look straight ahead on the road you wish me to tread, that I might not be tempted by any distraction. And make my eyes pure, that no false desires may be awakened within me.

Jakob Böhme (1575–1624) was first a shepherd and then a shoemaker in Germany. After his first work based on his visions of God was published, he was ordered by the Lutheran Church to stop writing. Böhme continued to write devotional books, which had far-reaching influence on thinkers as different as G. W. F. Hegel, Friedrich Schelling, and Isaac Newton.

teach me to pray

᧡ HENRI J. M. NOUWEN ᧡

Every day I see again that only you can teach me to pray, only you can set my heart at rest, only you can let me dwell in your presence. No book, no idea, no concept or theory will ever bring me close to you unless you yourself are the one who lets these instruments become the way to you.

But Lord, let me at least remain open to your initiative; let me wait patiently and attentively for that hour when you will come and break through all the walls I have erected. Teach me, O Lord, to pray. Amen.

Born in the Netherlands, Henri Nouwen (1932–96) was a priest, a professor, and the author of such books as *The Genesee Diary, The Wounded Healer, The Road to Daybreak,* and *Creative Ministry*. He taught at the University of Notre Dame, Yale Divinity School, and Harvard Divinity School. His autobiographical and meditative writings are regarded as among the most inspirational works of our time.

give me the listening ear

ar HOWARD THURMAN ar

Give me the listening ear. I seek this day the ear that will not shrink from the word that corrects and admonishes—the word that holds up before me the image of myself that causes me to pause and reconsider—the word that challenges me to deeper consecration and higher resolve—the word that lays bare needs that make my own days uneasy, that seizes upon every good, decent impulse of my nature, channeling it into paths of healing in the lives of others.

Give me the listening ear. I seek this day the disciplined mind, the disciplined heart, the disciplined life that makes my ear the focus of attention through which I may become mindful of expressions of life foreign to my own. I seek the stimulation that lifts me out of old ruts and established habits which keep me conscious of my self, my needs, my personal interests.

Give me this day—the eye that is willing to see the meaning of the ordinary, the familiar, the commonplace—the eye that is willing to see my own faults for what they are—the eye that is willing to see the likable qualities in those I may not like—the mistake in what I thought was correct—the strength in what I had labeled as weakness. Give me the eye that is willing to see that you have not left yourself without a witness in every living thing. Thus to walk with reverence and sensitivity through all the days of my life.

Give me the listening ear.
The eye that is willing to see.

Raised by his grandmother (a former slave), Howard Thurman (1900–81) became a Baptist minister and a leader in the civil rights movements of the 1950s and 1960s. He was the first African American to receive a full-time faculty appointment at Boston University. He authored more than twenty books on religion and race, including *Deep River: An Interpretation of Negro Spirituals, The Creative Encounter,* and *Apostles of Sensitiveness.*

enliven our minds,
inspire our conversation

∽ IONA COMMUNITY ∾

Throughout this day,
enliven our minds,
inspire our conversation,
inform our decisions,
and protect those we love.
And should today bring
what we neither anticipate nor desire,
increase our faith and decrease our pride
until we know that,
when we face the unexpected,
we do not stand alone.

Hear these prayers
made in the presence and in the name
of Jesus Christ our Lord.
Amen.

The Iona Community, composed of more than 240 members, is an ecumenical community of Christians working for social and political change and encouraging more inclusive approaches to worship. The Iona Community continues to welcome pilgrims to its island home off the coast of Scotland.

prayers for understanding

∾ JOHN CALVIN ∾

May the Lord grant that we may engage in contemplating the mysteries of his heavenly wisdom with really increasing devotion, to his glory and to our edification. Amen.

O Lord, who is the fountain of all wisdom and learning, you have given me the years of my youth to learn the arts and skills necessary for an honest and holy life. Enlighten my mind, that I may acquire knowledge. Strengthen my memory that I may retain what I have learnt. Govern my heart, that I may always be eager and diligent in my studies. And let your Spirit of truth, judgement and prudence guide my understanding, that I may perceive how everything I learn fits into your holy plan for the world.

Swiss theologian John Calvin (1509–64) was a driving force for the Protestant Reformation in Europe. His *Institutes of the Christian Religion* (1536) established the foundation for the Reformed tradition within Protestantism. Calvin would often begin his lectures in Geneva with the first of these two prayers.

prayer before study

~ THEODORE ROETHKE ~

Constricted by my tortured thought,
I am too centered on this spot.

So caged and cadged, so close within
A coat of unessential skin,

I would put off myself and flee
My inaccessibility.

A fool can play at being solemn
Revolving on his spinal column.

Deliver me, O Lord, from all
Activity centripetal.

Educated at the University of Michigan, Theodore Roethke
(1908–63) received numerous awards for his poetry, including the
Pulitzer Prize, the Bollingen Prize, and the National Book Award.
Writing to fellow poet John Ciardi in 1950, Roethke confided,
"I believe that to go forward as a spiritual man, it is necessary to
go back."

help me to concentrate

MICHAEL HOLLINGS
AND ETTA GULLICK

Lord, help me to concentrate on the work that I am about to do. Don't let me fritter my time away with idle thoughts, and help me really to get into things instead of just learning superficially. Keep my mind open to the thoughts of others, no matter how different from my own. You understand everything, everybody, and listen to everything. Help me to be open, more like you; make my understanding and sympathy more like yours.

Father Michael Hollings (1921–97) was a parish priest in England who lived simply and was known for his compassionate ministry to the poor and the homeless. He served for a number of years as a chaplain to Roman Catholic students at Oxford University.

Etta Gullick taught history and geographical discovery at Oxford as well as spirituality at St. Stephen's House, an Anglican theological college. Her students at St. Stephen's House affectionately referred to her prayer seminars as "Pray Better with Etta."

for true knowledge

◦— SUSANNA WESLEY —◦

Almighty God, I have found that to know Thee only as a philosopher; to have the most sublime and curious speculations concerning Thine essence, Thine attributes, Thy providence; to be able to demonstrate Thy being from all or any of the works of nature and to discourse with the greatest elegancy and propriety of words of Thine existence or operations, will avail me nothing, unless at the same time I know Thee experimentally: unless my heart perceive and know Thee to be its supreme good, its only happiness; unless my soul feel and acknowledge that she can find no repose, no peace, no joy, but in loving and being beloved by Thee; and does accordingly rest in Thee as the center of her being, the fountain of her pleasure, the origin of all virtue and goodness, her light, her life, her strength, her all; everything she wants or wishes in this world and forever.

Thus let me ever know Thee, O God! I neither despise nor neglect the light of reason, nor that knowledge of Thee that may be collected from this goodly system of created things, but this speculative knowledge is not the knowledge I want and wish for above all other. Teach me Thy way, O Lord! Amen.

Born in London, Susanna Wesley (1669–1742) wrote many letters of guidance to other Christians and to members of her family, including her sons John and Charles Wesley, the founders of Methodism.

prayer before class begins

∽ SARAH KLOS ∼

O Lord, our class is about to begin. Some of us are out of breath. Some of us are worried about all the things we left at home to do. And some of us couldn't care less—about the work we left at home or the work we have to do here in this class.

Slow us down, Lord. Ease the rush of our thoughts. Put our minds on you. Make us stop and think why we are here.

Do you ever speak to us through our parents, friends, our pastor, our teachers? Why?

Do you have something to tell us? If you do, help us to be ready to listen, ready to hear, ready to share ideas and thoughts, ready to learn, ready to teach with our lives. Amen.

Sarah Klos served as a director of Christian education with the Evangelical Lutheran Church in America for twenty-five years. She is the coauthor of *Sharing God's Mission in the Classroom* as well as the author of *Prayers: Alone / Together.*

lord, broaden our ideas

~ ORIGEN ~

Let us ask the Lord to broaden our ideas, make them clearer, and bring them nearer to the truth, that we may understand the other things too that he has revealed to his prophets. May we study the Holy Spirit's writings under the guidance of the Spirit himself and compare one spiritual interpretation with another, so that our explanation of the texts may be worthy of God and the Holy Spirit, who inspired them. May we do this through Christ Jesus, our Lord, to whom glory and power belong and will belong through all the ages. Amen.

Born in Alexandria, Egypt, Origen (185–254) was raised by Christian parents. His father was killed in the persecution of Alexandria in 202, and Origen was kept from seeking martyrdom by his mother, who hid his clothes. He was well known as a preacher and writer, and he founded a school at Caesarea in 231. Most of his theological works have been lost, but his most important work is considered to be *De principiis*. In 250 he was imprisoned and tortured; he survived only a few years after that.

prayer for understanding

~ ST. HILARY OF POITIERS ~

Almighty God, bestow upon us the meaning of words, the light of understanding, the nobility of diction and the faith of the true nature. And grant that what we believe we may also speak.

Hilary (c.315–67), bishop of Poitiers, was a convert from Neoplatonism and was involved in the Arian disputes, for which he was exiled for four years to Phrygia. He was the most respected Latin theologian of his day, renowned for defending the human and divine natures of Jesus. His feast day, January 13, gives his name to the spring term at the Law Courts and at Oxford and Durham universities in England.

the elixir

ᕽ GEORGE HERBERT ᕽ

Teach me, my God and King,
In all things thee to see,
And what I do in any thing,
To do it as for thee.

Not rudely, as a beast.
To run into an action;
But still to make thee prepossest
And give it his perfection.

A man that looks on glass,
On it may stay his eye;
Or if he pleaseth, through it pass,
And then the heav'n espy.

All may of thee partake:
Nothing can be so mean.
Which with this tincture (for thy sake)
Will not grow bright and clean.

A servant with this clause
Makes drudgery divine:
Who sweeps a room as for thy laws,
Makes that and th' action fine.

This is the famous stone
That turneth all to gold:
For that which God doth touch and own
Cannot for less be told.

George Herbert (1593–1633) received his B.A. and M.A. from Cambridge University, but struggled for a number of years to find his career. At the age of 37, he accepted a position at a small country church near Salisbury, England, where he preached and wrote poetry until his untimely death from tuberculosis three years later. Today, Herbert's poetry is regarded among the finest in the Christian literary tradition.

come to me in my mind

∾ HERBERT BROKERING ∾

Lord, ideas keep coming into my head,
and I don't know where they come from.
They seem to come from deep inside myself,
and they also come from the outside.
In me there lives so much that is new and original,
I'm glad for the gift of new thoughts.
Remind me this day of the importance of the
    human mind.
I am responsible;
I am imaginative.
Come to me in my mind, Jesus.

The Reverend Herbert Brokering was a pastor with the Evangelical Lutheran Church in America. He has written a number of books, including *The Night before Jesus, Wholly Holy, A Pilgrimage to Luther's Germany,* and *In a Promise.* Rev. Brokering lives in Minneapolis.

the speaking voice

◦— A. W. TOZER —◦

Lord, teach me to listen. The times are noisy and my ears are weary with the thousand raucous sounds which continuously assault them. Give me the spirit of the boy Samuel when he said to Thee, "Speak, for thy servant heareth." Let me hear Thee speaking in my heart. Let me get used to the sound of Thy Voice, that its tones may be familiar when the sounds of earth die away and the only sound will be the music of Thy speaking Voice. Amen.

Aiden Wilson Tozer (1897–1963) had neither a college nor a seminary education, yet he served for most of his life as a pastor in the Christian and Missionary Alliance, became the editor of *The Alliance Witness*, and authored more than a dozen books. He has been described as an evangelical mystic with a passion for truth. He wrote, "Perception of ideas rather than the storing of them should be the aim of education. The mind should be an eye to see with rather than a bin to store facts in." And, he believed, there is "nothing more wonderful than an alert and eager mind made incandescent by the presence of the indwelling Christ."

prayer

～ C. S. LEWIS ～

Master, they say that when I seem
    To be in speech with you,
Since you make no replies, it's all a dream
    —One talker aping two.

They are half right, but not as they
    Imagine; rather I
Seek in myself the things I meant to say,
    And lo! the wells are dry.

Then, seeing me empty, you forsake
    The Listener's role, and through
My dead lips breathe and into utterance wake
    The thoughts I never knew.

Clive Staples Lewis (1898–1963), professor of English literature at the universities of Oxford and Cambridge, became one of the most popular defenders of Christianity in the twentieth century. He is best known for his apologetic works *Mere Christianity* and *The Screwtape Letters* and for his children's fantasies, *The Chronicles of Narnia*.

create in us a passion for truth

∽ STANLEY HAUERWAS ∾

True God of True God, create in us a passion for truth. Make us lust for, long for, taste, feel, roll in the grass of your love, your truth. Free us from the fear of truth by making us God-fearers. May we hate all that which would tempt us to settle for the greatest of all lies, the half-truth. So formed, give us simple speech, graceful speech, lovely speech, so that we might truthfully speak to one another, that we might love one another in truth. Honor us with honesty that we might be honorable and, thus, trustworthy people. Oh! We so long to be capable of trust. We are so tired, so bored, by our cynicism. So yes, dear Lord, we pray that you will make us truthful servants so that we may say to ourselves and one another, "You can trust me." Amen.

Stanley Hauerwas was born in Texas, raised among Methodists, and studied at Yale University and the University of Edinburgh. He is now professor of theological ethics at the Divinity School, Duke University. Dr. Hauerwas is the author of many books, including *The Peaceable Kingdom: A Primer in Christian Ethics* (1983), *Christians among the Virtues* (1997), and *Wilderness Wanderings: Probing Twentieth-Century Theology* (1997).

take, o lord, and receive

USED BY MOTHER TERESA AND THE MISSIONARIES OF CHARITY

Take, O Lord, and receive
All my liberty, my memory,
My understanding and my will,
All that I have and possess.
You have given them to me;
To you, O Lord, I restore them.
All things are yours:
Dispose of them according to your will.
Give me your love and your grace,
For this is enough for me.

Founder of the Society of the Missionaries of Charity in 1948, Mother Teresa (1910–97) worked in the slums of Calcutta and in other cities, living out her love of Christ. She once wrote, "My poor ones in the world's slums are like the suffering Christ. In them God's Son lives and dies, and through them God shows me his true face." She received the Nobel Peace Prize in 1979. This prayer, while not directly composed by Mother Teresa, is regularly used by the Missionaries of Charity.

CHAPTER 3

PRAYERS IN TIMES OF
SUCCESS AND FAILURE

Growth and learning demand risk. Anytime we set about learning—whether we're reading a challenging book, embarking on a degree program, composing a paper, or writing a lecture—we expose ourselves to the possibility of failure. Risk is frightening but necessary because, as Eric Milner-White suggests, we do not have "knowledge enough to need no learning, wisdom enough to need no correction." The prayers in this chapter help us as we bolster our courage to face new challenges.

Learning and growth may seem hazardous for those who have failed, who need to forgive themselves so that they can begin to grow again. These prayers seek divine resources, so that those who fail may determine not to play it safe.

But risk can also be hard for those who have

known success. Our culture encourages expertise; we are often expected to do only what we know we can do easily and well. Often the successful suffer from fear of failure, afraid that what they say might not be profound or that they might lose their high class standing. They need some divine pressure to step out and try some new area of study.

In fact, the difficulty of risk may be common to all of us whether we have (largely) failed or succeeded. It has to do with our sense of who we are. Most of us have heard the imposter syndrome's sinister whisper: "Your understanding, your degree, your enjoyment in learning—they were all a fluke, a mistake!"

What we need is a sense of divine perspective, much as Joseph Bernardin prayed for: "When we do well in work and play, give us a sense of proportion." Failure is inevitable when we risk. When our fear of failure cripples us from taking further risk, or when we find our sense of self totally entangled in success, we face danger, unwholeness, and loss of balance.

Left to ourselves, we easily cave in to pressures and lose perspective. We struggle to look honestly at our failures and our successes—we despair or we gloat. In this chapter we bring God both our successes and our failures, and we ask for clear vision as we continue to accept challenges and as we resolve to strive for perfection of effort rather than perfection of performance.

christ, the master carpenter

∽ IONA COMMUNITY ∼

O Christ, the Master Carpenter
Who, at the last, through wood and nails,
Purchased our whole salvation.
Wield well your tools in the workshop of your world,
So that we, who come rough-hewn to your bench,
May here be fashioned to a truer beauty of your hand.
We ask it for your own name's sake.

The Iona Community was founded in 1938 by George MacLeod on the island by the same name off the coast of Scotland. Its many members also seek to live their common life in the midst of violence in various urban centers.

prayer in time of failure

ᴕ W. E. B. DU BOIS ᴕ

O, God, teach us to know that failure is as much a part of life as success—and whether it shall be evil or good depends upon the way we meet it—if we face it listlessly and daunted, angrily or vengefully, then indeed is it evil for it spells death. But if we let our failures stand as guideposts and as warnings—as beacons and as guardians—then is honest failure far better than stolen success, and but a part of that great training which God gives us to make us women and men. The race is not to the swift—nor the battle to the strong, O God. Amen.

Educated at Fisk University, Harvard University, and the University of Berlin, W. E. B. Du Bois (1868–1963) was the first African American to receive a doctorate from Harvard. A prolific author of novels, autobiographical sketches, verses, and scholarly studies, including his monumental work *The Souls of Black Folk*, Du Bois served as professor of economics and sociology at Atlanta University.

making possible

∾ AMY CARMICHAEL ∾

May thy grace, O Lord, make that possible to me which seems impossible to me by nature.

Born to a prominent family in northern Ireland, Amy Carmichael (1867–1951) served as a Keswick missionary to India for more than half a century. There she devoted her efforts to rescuing children from temple prostitution. Although she suffered from crippling arthritis after her retirement, she wrote many popular devotional books, including *Things as They Are, The Beginning of a Story,* and *Lotus Buds*.

for faith and for hope

∽ SØREN KIERKEGAARD ∽

Teach me, O God, not to torture myself, not to make a martyr out of myself through stifling reflection, but rather teach me to breathe deeply in faith.

O Lord, my God, give me again the courage to hope. Merciful God, let hope once again make fertile my sterile and barren mind.

Søren Kierkegaard (1813–55), who lived his whole life at Copenhagen, Denmark, was the son of a wealthy Lutheran businessman. Always a melancholy man, he is best known for his theological and philosophical writings, which influenced existentialist thinkers as well as theologians like Karl Barth. His more religious books, such as *Christian Discourses and Training in Christianity,* show a deep understanding of the cross.

acknowledging our need

~ ERIC MILNER-WHITE ~

Suffer me never to think
    that I have knowledge enough to need no teaching,
        wisdom enough to need no correction,
        talents enough to need no grace,
        goodness enough to need no progress,
        humility enough to need no repentance,
        devotion enough to need no quickening,
        strength sufficient without thy Spirit;
    lest, standing still, I fall back for evermore.

Eric Milner-White (1884–1964) was dean of York in England. He founded the Oratory of the Good Shepherd, an Anglican order of priests. He is the author of a number of prayers, hymns, and books, including *One God and Father of All* and *My God, My Glory.*

for light in times of darkness

◠— HILDEGARD OF BINGEN —◠

The Word made flesh for us gives us the greatest hope
that the murky night of darkness will not overwhelm us,
but we shall see the daylight of eternity.

Lord, let us receive your clear light;
be for us such a mirror of light
that we may be given grace to see you unendingly.
If we are overcome, you have the power to forgive us:
therefore, in my sin I call on you, my Light, for help,
for you were sent into the world
to enlighten my heart, to nurture true repentance,
and to make the Holy Spirit's work grow powerfully
    in me.
With the Father and the Holy Spirit
you live and reign for ever!

From the age of three, Hildegard (1098–1179) had visions of
"living light." She became head of a Benedictine congregation in
1136. Known for her healing and preaching, she founded several
communities and wrote several books.

the apologist's evening prayer

᠊᠊ C. S. LEWIS ᠊᠊

From all my lame defeats and oh! much more
From all the victories that I seemed to score;
From cleverness shot forth on Thy behalf
At which, while angels weep, the audience laugh;
From all my proofs of Thy divinity,
Thou, who wouldst give no sign, deliver me.

Thoughts are but coins. Let me trust, instead
Of Thee, their thin-worn image of Thy head.
From all my thoughts, even from my thoughts of Thee,
O thou fair Silence, fall, and set me free.
Lord of the narrow gate and the needle's eye,
Take from me all my trumpery lest I die.

Best known for his children's fantasies, *The Chronicles of Narnia*, Clive Staples Lewis (1898–1963) was professor of English literature at the universities of Oxford and Cambridge. He became one of the most popular defenders of Christianity in the twentieth century and also wrote a number of popular works on theological subjects, such as suffering and prayer.

spinning tops

∽ KATHY KEAY ∼

How strange—
we are all so ardent in our piety
so careful not to slip up
so intent on making our individual lives
count in the scheme of things
tyrannized by overfull diaries
driven by the echo of our 'well done'.
And where does it all lead?

Spinning round like tops
we spiral down before You
in now grubby, tattered clothes
out of breath.

Deal gently with us, Lord.

Kathy Keay studied English and education at Oxford and then worked as a freelance writer, editor, and journalist. She traveled widely, presenting workshops in the United Kingdom, the United States, India, Africa, and South Africa. The author of eight books, she died in 1994.

for a sense of proportion

~ JOSEPH L. BERNARDIN ~

Grant unto us, O Lord, the gift of modesty. When we speak, teach us to give our opinion quietly and sincerely. When we do well in work or play, give us a sense of proportion, that we be neither unduly elated nor foolishly self-deprecatory. Help us in success to realize what we owe to thee and to the efforts of others: in failure, to avoid dejection; and in all ways to be simple and natural, quiet in manner and lowly in thought: through Christ.

Born of Italian immigrant parents, Joseph L. Bernardin (1928–96) grew up in South Carolina and felt a call to the priesthood when he was in college. In 1982 he became the Roman Catholic cardinal of Chicago. He was a recipient of the Albert Einstein International Peace Prize and the author of many books.

in all our learning give us grace

⌒ E. J. BURNS ⌒

O God, you give to humankind
a searching heart and questing mind;
grant us to find your truth and laws,
and wisdom to perceive their cause.

In all our learning give us grace
to bow ourselves before your face;
as knowledge grows, Lord, keep us free
from self-destructive vanity.

Sometimes we think we understand
all workings of your mighty hand;
then through your Son help us to know
those truths which you alone can show.

Teach us to joy in things revealed,
to search with care all yet concealed;
as through Christ's light your truth we find
and worship you with heart and mind.

Educated at Liverpool and Oxford, E. J. Burns has always
lived in Lancashire, England. With special interests in biblical
studies, the relationship between science and theology, and ethi-
cal issues in medicine, he has pastored several churches and
served as a hospital chaplain for many years. He has written a
number of hymns.

lord, in my success i need you

✑ PETER MARSHALL ✑

Lord, forgive me that when life's circumstances lift me to the crest of the wave, I tend to forget Thee. Yet, like an errant child, I have blamed Thee with my every failure, even as I credit myself with every success.

When my fears evaporate like the morning mist, then vainly I imagine that I am sufficient unto myself, that material resources and human resources are enough.

I need Thee when the sun shines, lest I forget the storm and the dark. I need Thee when I am popular, when my friends and those who work beside me approve and compliment me. I need Thee more then, lest my head begin to swell.

O God, forgive me for my stupidity, my blindness in success, my lack of trust in Thee. Be Thou now my Saviour in success. Save me from conceit. Save me from pettiness. Save me from myself! And take this success, I pray, and use it for Thy glory. In Thy strength, I pray. Amen.

Peter Marshall (1902–49) emigrated from Scotland to the United States, where he trained as a Presbyterian minister and was, in 1947, made chaplain to the United States Senate. His life story was told by his wife, Catherine Marshall, in the book *A Man Called Peter*.

a prayer for contentment

᠙— JEREMY TAYLOR —᠙

O Almighty God, Father and Lord of all the creatures, by secret and undiscernible ways bringing good out of evil: give me wisdom from above; teach me to be content in all changes of person and condition, to be temperate in prosperity, and in adversity to be meek, patient, and resigned; and to look through the cloud, in the meantime doing my duty with an unwearied diligence, and an undisturbed resolution.

Jeremy Taylor (1613–67), an Anglican bishop and writer, was chaplain to Charles I. After the king's defeat, he escaped to Wales, where he wrote several books, including *The Rule and Exercises of Holy Living, The Rule and Exercises of Holy Dying,* and *The Golden Grove.* He became known for his deep spiritual insight.

looking back, looking ahead

∽ ALEKSANDR SOLZHENITSYN ∽

How easy it is to live with You, O Lord.
How easy to believe in You.
When my spirit is overwhelmed within me,
When even the keenest see no further than the night,
And know not what to do tomorrow,
You bestow on me the certitude
That You exist and are mindful of me,
That all the paths of righteousness are not barred.

As I ascend into the hill of earthly glory,
I turn back and gaze, astonished, on the road
That led me here beyond despair,
Where I too may reflect Your radiance upon mankind.

All that I may reflect, You shall accord me,
And appoint others where I shall fail.

Born in 1918, Aleksandr Solzhenitsyn received his training in science. Drafted into the Soviet Red Army in 1941, he was arrested and sent to prison in Siberia in 1945 for criticizing Stalin in a letter to a friend. He became internationally known in 1962 for his novel *One Day in the Life of Ivan Denisovich*. In 1970 he won the Nobel Prize for Literature, but the Soviet government refused to allow him to accept it. Forced into exile four years later, he lived in seclusion in the United States. The collapse of the Soviet Union eventually made it possible for him to return to Russia in 1994.

go to the root

~ EUGENE PETERSON ~

I am more comfortable, Father, with an image of you as a gentleman farmer, pruning an occasional branch and raking up a few leaves. But you go to the root. I submit myself to your surgery, and hope in your salvation. Amen.

Eugene Peterson, professor emeritus of spiritual theology at Regent College, is the author of numerous books, including *Run with the Horses: A Quest for Life at Its Best* and *Earth and Altar: The Community of Prayer in a Selfbound Society*. He spent many years as pastor of a Presbyterian church in Maryland.

the task your wisdom has assigned

∽ CHARLES WESLEY ∽

The task your wisdom has assigned
here let me cheerfully fulfill;
in all my work your presence find
and prove your good and perfect will.

You I would set at my right hand
where eyes my inmost secrets view.
And labor on at your command
and offer all my work to you.

Help me to bear your easy yoke
and every moment watch and pray
and still to things eternal look
and hasten to that glorious day.

Charles Wesley (1707–88) was born the eighteenth child in the family of Susanna and Samuel Wesley. After a missionary trip to Georgia, he returned to England, where he wrote more than fifty-five hundred hymns, including "Hark! The Herald Angels Sing," "O, for a Thousand Tongues," "Love Divine, All Loves Excelling," and "Christ the Lord Is Risen Today."

new beginning

∽ ERIC MILNER-WHITE ∾

O Lord God, make me die to the old life
    that I may begin the new.
Every good desire, all strong and tender purpose
    every inspiration to works of love,
        come from thee.
Thou art the beginning of my beginnings,
        well of my fresh springs,
    guide of their channels, guard of their banks,
        goal of their full stream,
        ocean of their rest.

Move me to seek and welcome thy will
    and submit to it willingly and wholly;
for that is the new and the perfect and the endless life,
        every day, every hour.
Thy mercies are new every morning;
        so be my obedience:

new be my fear of thee
    which is the beginning of wisdom;
new my prayer,
    school of my faith,
    university of divine learning,
    light of hope;
and new my love
    which is the crown of these,
    and life eternal.

In 1918, shortly after the armistice ending World War I, Eric Milner-White (1884–1964) introduced the popular service of Nine Lessons and Carols at King's College, Cambridge. Later the dean of York, he composed many prayers and hymns.

CHAPTER 4

PRAYERS IN TIMES OF STRESS AND UNCERTAINTY

Sometimes learning shakes us up.

Just when we feel secure—we understand the world and our faith pretty well—we take a plunge into learning and find ourselves gasping. We are out of our depth.

At the heart of real learning, miles away from rote memorization or superficial reading, is knowledge that affects us profoundly and touches us deeply. Here we will be changed.

Dazzled with possibilities, dizzied by challenges, we have lost what seemed unshakable. We may find ourselves wishing for "the good old days," only to find that the door has locked behind us.

The prayers in this chapter offer comfort for those who face the challenges and stresses of learning. They remind us that God knows that our quest for knowledge will stretch and extend us. They encourage us to keep pushing at the edges, to be filled with what Louis Untermeyer calls "buoyant doubt" so that we are willing to learn. These prayers reminds us that often the only way to peace and wisdom is found by taking the path marked "doubts and darkness," trusting that God is there.

This is what makes the Christian quest for wisdom different. Even when what we learn doesn't make sense or doesn't fit our categories, even when our certainties change, we can rest on the wisdom of the unchangeable God, who is there "upsetting our easiness / contradicting our compromises / replacing our narrow vision." What may appear to us like a step away from faith—a step that we fear will lead to a headlong tumble—is in fact a step of deeper faith. Here we learn to rest in the deep places of God and, as Kierkegaard suggests, "breathe deeply in faith."

Like Peter, who abandoned the refuge of the boat to walk toward Jesus, we abandon our securities and find ourselves face-to-face with ultimate comfort and profound security. We are reminded that Jesus didn't call himself the answer; he called himself the way.

free us from the need to justify ourselves

ᕦ— JANET MORLEY —ᕤ

O God, before whose face
we are not made righteous
even by being right;
free us from the need to justify ourselves
by our own anxious striving,
that we may be abandoned
to faith in you alone,
through Jesus Christ. Amen.

Janet Morley is author of many prayers that were collected in a worship anthology, *Celebrating Women*. Adult education adviser for the relief organization Christian Aid, she acted as editor for the collection *Bread of Tomorrow: Praying with the World's Poor.*

when our belief is perplexed by new learning

❧ GEORGE RIDDING ❧

In times of doubts and questionings, when our belief is perplexed by new learning, new teaching, new thought, when our faith is strained by creeds, by doctrines, by mysteries beyond our understanding, give us the faithfulness of learners and the courage of believers in You; give us boldness to examine, and faith to trust all truth; patience and insight to master difficulties; stability to hold fast our traditions with enlightened interpretations, to admit all fresh truth made known to us, and in times of trouble to grasp new knowledge and to combine it loyally and honestly with the old. Amen.

George Ridding (1828–1904) served as headmaster of Winchester College in England and as first bishop of the newly created diocese of Southwell. As an educator, he was known for his reforms and for his expansion of the curriculum. As bishop, he was known for his independent thought, and his advice was frequently sought by his superiors.

when our confidence is shaken

FRED PRATT GREEN

When our confidence is shaken
In beliefs we thought secure,
When the spirit in its sickness
Seeks but cannot find a cure,
God is active in the tensions
Of a faith not yet mature.

Solar systems, void of meaning,
Freeze the spirit into stone;
Always our researches lead us
To the ultimate unknown.
Faith must die, or come full circle
To its source in God alone.

In the discipline of praying,
When it's hardest to believe;
In the drudgery of caring,
When it's not enough to grieve;
Faith, maturing, learns acceptance
Of the insight we receive.

God is love, and thus redeems us
In the Christ we crucify;
This is God's eternal answer
To the world's eternal why.
May we in this faith maturing
Be content to live and die!

Fred Pratt Green (1903–2000), a Methodist pastor, started writing plays and poetry when he was in college, publishing three collections of poems. In his mid-sixties he started writing hymns, many of which have been collected in *The Hymns and Ballads of Fred Pratt Green*.

my doubting questions

∽— EUGENE PETERSON —∽

Instead of suppressing what I am curious about and avoiding the hard questions that get between me and you, O God, teach me how to submit them to your treatment. I want to bring my doubting questions as well as my faithful obedience into your presence. Amen.

Well known for his books, including *Working the Angles: The Shape of Pastoral Integrity* and *The Contemplative Pastor*, Eugene Peterson is professor emeritus of spiritual theology at Regent College.

not certainty, but joy

∽ STANLEY HAUERWAS ∾

True God of all Truths, how we desire certainty amid the confusion of our lives. We think we could make it if we just had one thing we could know without doubt, one way to be that was not ambiguous, one other we could unreservedly trust. Yet all such knowledge, being and trust too often reflect our desperation rather than your glory. We pray, therefore, not for certainty but for joy at the discernment that you have discovered us and given us a way to go on in the midst of confusion. For what more could we ask? Amen.

Stanley Hauerwas, professor of theological ethics at the Divinity School, Duke University, is regarded as one of the most influential religious thinkers of our day. His work cuts across various disciplines, including theology, philosophy, and sociology. He is a prolific author of such books as *The Peaceable Kingdom: A Primer in Christian Ethics* (1983) and *In Good Company: The Church as Polis* (1995).

you don't have to choose up sides

∾ MARJORIE HOLMES ∾

God, it does not help my faith to be with blind and credulous people who have inherited their religion. Or whose beliefs are package-mixed and who accept you only because they have never questioned you, because they do not think.

In many ways they are worse than the skeptics, the agnostics and atheists who doubt you or deny you altogether.

I cannot abide dumb or bigoted people. I want to flee to the intellectuals. I want to be on the side of people who at least have some logical reasons for what they think.

Lord, help me to remember that I don't have to choose up sides. That my own faith has nothing to do with either kind of people.

Faith is my own private need of you reaching out to find you.

Faith is my own intelligence responding to yours.

My faith is my knowledge that in your vast intelligence you created this world—and me.

My faith is my growing conviction that you are not off somewhere running the universe, but here, now, with me. That you care about me.

Thank you for this faith.

Born in 1910, columnist Marjorie Holmes taught writing courses at several universities and has long been associated with the Georgetown University Writers Conference. She is the author of many books, including *I've Got to Talk to Somebody, God.*

we need your forgiveness

We need your forgiveness, merciful God,
For not allowing our complacency to be shattered,
For taking refuge too often in the familiar and the
    certain,
For not believing in the victory of vulnerability,
For not daring to accept your gifts nor claim your
    promises.
Grant us true repentance.
Set us free to hear your word to us.
Set us free to serve you.

The St. Hilda Community, which takes its name from Hilda
of Whitby (614–80), was founded in 1987 in London, with a particular aim to promote women's ministry. This prayer appears in
their publication, *Women Included: A Book of Services and Prayers.*

the craving for certainty

∽ JIM COTTER ∾

Spirit of Wisdom,
take from us all fuss,
the clattering of noise,
the temptation to dominate by the power of words,
the craving for certainty.
Lead us through the narrow gate of not knowing,
that we may listen and obey,
and come to a place of stillness,
of true conversation and wisdom.

Jim Cotter, author of several books on prayer, including *Psalms of a Pilgrim People, Prayer in the Morning,* and *Prayer at Night*, lives in Sheffield, England, and is well known as a lecturer and retreat leader.

teach me to be silent

↜ HENRI J. M. NOUWEN ↝

O Lord Jesus, your words to your Father were born out of your silence. Lead me into this silence, so that my words may be spoken in your name and thus be fruitful. It is so hard to be silent, silent with my mouth, but even more, silent with my heart. There is so much talking going on within me. It seems that I am always involved in inner debates with myself, my friends, my enemies, my supporters, my opponents, my colleagues, and my rivals. But this inner debate reveals how far my heart is from you. If I were simply to rest at your feet and realize that I belong to you and you alone, I would easily stop arguing with all the real and imagined people around me. These arguments show my insecurity, my fear, my apprehensions, and my need for being recognized and receiving attention. You, O Lord, will give me all the attention I need if I would simply stop talking and start listening to you. I know that in the silence of my heart you will speak to me and show me your love. Give me, O Lord, that silence. Let me be patient and grow slowly into this silence in which I can be with you. Amen.

Well known for such books as *Out of Solitude*, *In the Name of Jesus*, and *The Way of the Desert*, Henri Nouwen (1932–96) was a priest, professor, and writer. Born in the Netherlands, he taught at the University of Notre Dame, Yale Divinity School, and Harvard Divinity School. In his later years he made his home in L'Arche Community in Canada.

flickering mind

∼ DENISE LEVERTOV ∼

Lord, not you,
it is I who am absent.
At first
belief was a joy I kept in secret,
stealing alone
into sacred places:
a quick glance, and away—and back,
circling.
I have long since uttered your name
but now
I elude your presence.
I stop
to think about you, and my mind
at once
like a minnow darts away,
darts
into the shadows, into gleams that fret
unceasing over
the river's purling and passing.
Not for one second
will my self hold still, but wanders
anywhere,
everywhere it can turn. Not you,
it is I am absent.

You are the stream, the fish, the light,
the pulsing shadow,
you the unchanging presence, in whom all
moves and changes.
How can I focus my flickering, perceive
at the fountain's heart
the sapphire I know is there?

American poet Denise Levertov (1923–97) was born in England to a Welsh mother and a Jewish father who had converted to Christianity but maintained a vibrant interest in Hasidism. Denise Levertov became well known as a political poet during the Vietnam War. Her later poems began to express her Christian faith more overtly.

dear lord and father of mankind

~ JOHN GREENLEAF WHITTIER ~

Dear Lord and Father of mankind,
Forgive our foolish ways!
Reclothe us in our rightful mind;
In purer lives Thy service find,
In deeper reverence, praise.

Drop Thy still dews of quietness,
Till all our strivings cease;
Take from our souls the strain and stress,
And let our ordered lives confess
The beauty of Thy peace.

Breathe through the heats of our desire
Thy coolness and Thy balm;
Let sense be dumb, let flesh retire;
Speak through the earthquake, wind and fire,
O still small voice of calm!

John Greenleaf Whittier (1807–92) grew up in a Quaker family on a farm in Massachusetts. He published his first poem at age nineteen, but most of his energies were directed toward the abolition of slavery as he wrote and edited various antislavery publications. When his masterpiece, "Snow-Bound," appeared in 1866, Whittier achieved national recognition. Many of his poems are no longer read, but a number of his fine hymns endure.

be present in our past, o lord

∽ JEANNETTE LINDHOLM ∾

Lord, you have welcomed us; we come
To pray for healing in your love.
Please, as we wait to meet you here,
All doubts, impediments remove.

Redeem our sorrows; let our tears
Become your healing waters blessed.
And lead us, lost, to quiet streams
Where we shall find ourselves refreshed.

Be present in our past, O Lord,
And in the mem'ry of our days.
When terrors of the night oppress,
Protect us in your strong embrace.

Remind us of your faithfulness,
The promise of your presence, Lord.
And keep us trusting in your grace
Until we greet you whole, restored.

Educated at Concordia College (Moorhead, Minnesota), Indiana University, and the University of Minnesota, Jeannette Lindholm now teaches in the English department at Salem State College in Salem, Massachusetts.

i need thy sense of time

∾— HOWARD THURMAN —∾

I Need Thy Sense of Time.
> Always I have an underlying anxiety about things.
> Sometimes I am in a hurry to achieve my ends
> And am completely without patience. It is hard
> > for me to realize
>
> That some growth is slow,
> That all processes are not swift. I cannot always
> > discriminate
>
> Between what takes time to develop and what can
> > be rushed,
>
> Because my sense of time is dulled.
> I measure things in terms of happenings.
> Oh to understand the meaning of perspective
> That I may do all things with a profound sense of
> > leisure—of time.

I Need Thy Sense of Order.
> The confusion of the details of living
> Is sometimes overwhelming. The little things
> Keep getting in my way providing ready-made

Excuses for failure to do and be
What I know I ought to do and be.
Much time is spent on things that are not very
    important
While significant things are put into an
    insignificant place
In my scheme of order. I must unscramble
    my affairs
So that my life will become order. O God,
    I need thy sense of order.

I Need Thy Sense of the Future.
    Teach me to know that life is ever
    On the side of the future.
    Keep alive in me the forward look, the high hope,
    The onward surge. Let me not be frozen
    Either by the past or the present.
    Grant me, O patient Father, thy sense of
        the future
    Without which all life would sicken and die.

Raised by his grandmother (a former slave), Howard
Thurman (1900–81) helped to organize the interracial Church for
the Fellowship of All Peoples in San Francisco. He wrote more
than twenty books on religion and race. His work significantly
influenced Martin Luther King Jr.

invitation to ambiguity

℘— EUGENE PETERSON —℘

I like neat, black-and-white solutions to life, Lord, but the existence you invite me into is ambiguous: there is the miracle of Isaac, but there is also the fact of Ishmael. Like Sarah I would like to banish what doesn't fit into my scheme; but your scheme is larger than mine. Show me how to live in your larger providence. Amen.

The pastor of a church for many years, Eugene Peterson is now professor emeritus of spiritual theology at Regent College in Vancouver, British Columbia. He is the author of numerous books, including *The Message*.

searching for faith

◦— RICHARD J. FOSTER —◦

God, today I resonate with the desperate cry in the Gospel, "I believe, help my unbelief." Sometimes I think I operate my life out of more doubt than faith. And yet I want to believe . . . and I do believe.

I'm a complex creature. At times I can believe with my head, while my body is still locked into patterns of skepticism and doubt. Faith is not yet in my muscles, my bones, my glands.

Increase faith within me, O Lord. I'm sure that for faith to grow you will put me in situations where I'll need resources beyond myself. I submit to this process.

Will this mean moving out on behalf of others, praying for them and trusting you to work in them? If so, then show me the who, what, when, and where, and I will seek to act at your bidding. Throughout I am trusting you to take me from faith to faith—from the faith I do have to the faith that I am in the process of receiving.

Thank you for hearing my prayer.

Amen.

A writer and teacher, Richard Foster is best known for his writing on the spiritual disciplines, including *The Celebration of Discipline, Freedom of Simplicity,* and *Prayer*. He writes, "Superficiality is the curse of our age. . . . The desperate need today is not for a greater number of intelligent, or gifted people, but for deep people."

keep me in the hollow of your hand

∽ BROTHER RAMON ∽

Lord of the elements and changing seasons, keep me in the hollow of your hand. When I am tossed to and fro with the winds of adversity and the blasts of sickness and misunderstanding, still my racing heart, quiet my troubled mind.

Bring me at last through the storms and tribulations of this mortal life into the calm evening of your unchanging love; and grant that in the midst of my present perplexities and confusion I may experience your peace which passes human understanding.

With spiritual roots in the Baptist church, the late Brother Ramon (d. 1999) became a member of the Anglican Society of St. Francis. He conducted many spiritual retreats and was the author of such books as *The Wisdom of St. Francis, The Heart of Prayer,* and *The Prayer Mountain: Exploring the High Places of Prayer.*

prayers of steel

∽ CARL SANDBURG ∽

Lay me on an anvil, O God.
Beat me and hammer me into a crowbar.
Let me pry loose old walls.
Let me lift and loosen old foundations.

Lay me on an anvil, O God.
Beat me and hammer me into a steel spike.
Drive me into the girders that hold a
    skyscraper together.
Take red-hot rivets and fasten me into the
    central girders.
Let me be the great nail holding a skyscraper
    through blue nights into white stars.

Born in Galesburg, Illinois, into a poor but affectionate family of Swedish immigrants, Carl Sandburg (1878–1967) found employment as a migratory laborer, dishwasher, porter, brick maker, and salesman. While working as a reporter for a Chicago newspaper, he became popular as a poet of middle America. His poems often express the voice of a common individual confronted by the complexities of modern life. Sandburg was also well known for his *Rootabaga Stories* for children and for a major biography of Abraham Lincoln.

i have not knowledge

↶ GEORGE MACDONALD ↷

I have not knowledge, wisdom, insight, thought,
    Nor understanding, fit to justify
Thee in Thy work, O Perfect! Thou hast brought
Me up to this; and lo! what Thou has wrought,
    I cannot comprehend. But I can cry,
    "O enemy, the Maker hath not done;
One day thou shalt behold, and from the sight
    shalt run."

Thou workest perfectly. And if it seem
    Some things are not so well, 'tis but because
        They are too loving deep, too lofty wise,
    For me, poor child, to understand their laws.
My highest wisdom, half is but a dream;
My love runs helpless like a falling stream;
    Thy good embraces ill, and lo! its illness dies.

George MacDonald (1824–1905) was born in Scotland and trained for the ministry in Aberdeen. After losing his first post on suspicion of heresy, he turned to writing. He wrote a number of children's books, novels, and more theological works such as *Unspoken Sermons*. About MacDonald, C. S. Lewis once said, "I know hardly any other writer who seems to be closer, or more continually close, to the Spirit of Christ Himself."

prayer of a divided heart

⌒ COUNTEE CULLEN ⌒

Jesus of the twice-turned cheek,
Lamb of God, although I speak
With my mouth thus, in my heart
Do I play a double part.
Ever at Thy glowing altar
Must my heart grow sick and falter,
Wishing He I served were black,
Thinking then it would not lack
Precedent of pain to guide it,
Let who would or might deride it;
Surely then this flesh would know
Yours had borne a kindred woe.
Lord, I fashion dark gods, too,
Daring even to give You
Dark despairing features where,
Crowned with dark rebellious hair,
Patience wavers just so much as
Mortal grief compels, while touches
Quick and hot, of anger, rise
To smitten cheek and weary eyes.
Lord, forgive me if my need
Sometimes shapes a human creed.

Countee Cullen (1903–46) grew up in Harlem, the son of a minister to an African Methodist Church. He graduated from New York University and from Harvard. His first book of poetry, *Color,* appeared when he was a college senior.

the doubter's prayer

∽— ANNE BRONTË —∾

Eternal power, of earth and air!
　　Unseen, yet seen in all around;
Remote, but swelling everywhere;
　　Though silent heard in every sound;

If e'er thine ear in Mercy lent,
　　When wretched mortals cried to Thee,
And if indeed, Thy Son was sent,
　　To save lost sinners such as me:

Then hear me now, while kneeling here,
　　I life to Thee my heart and eye,
And all my soul ascends in prayer,
　　Oh, give me—Give me Faith! I cry.

While Faith is with me, I am blest;
　　It turns my darkest night to day;
But while I clasp it to my breast,
　　I often feel it slide away.

Anne Brontë (1820–49), like her more famous sisters, Emily and Charlotte, was a successful writer of fiction. The youngest child in the Brontë family, Anne was educated mainly at the parsonage in Haworth, England. She is best remembered for her novels *Agnes Grey* and *The Tenant of Wildfell Hall.*

from one discovery to another

⌒ ROGER SCHUTZ ⌒

Although within us there are wounds,
Lord Christ, above all there is
the miracle of your mysterious presence.
Thus, made lighter or even set free,
we are going with you, the Christ,
from one discovery to another.

Roger Schutz sheltered Jews and other refugees in the village of Taizé, France, during the 1940s. In 1944 he formed an ecumenical monastic community that attracts thousands of pilgrims each year. Brother Roger is the author of a number of vigorous prayers and meditations.

afraid to trust you

∽ A. W. TOZER ∽

Father, I want to know Thee, but my coward heart fears to give up its toys. I cannot part with them without inward bleeding, and I do not try to hide from Thee the terror of the parting. I come trembling, but I do come. Please root from my heart all those things which I have cherished so long, and which have become a very part of my living self, so that Thou mayest enter and dwell there without a rival. Then shalt Thou make the place of Thy feet glorious. Then shall my heart have not need of the sun to shine in it, for Thyself wilt be the light of it, and there shall be no night there.

Aiden Wilson Tozer (1897–1963) authored a number of books, including *The Pursuit of God* and *The Knowledge of the Holy.* A rather quiet man, he was known for his prayerful life. He once said, "When we become too glib in prayer, we are most surely talking to ourselves."

god, keep me still unsatisfied

∾ LOUIS UNTERMEYER ∾

God, though this life is but a wraith,
    Although we know not what we use,
Although we grope with little faith,
    Give me the heart to fight—and lose.

Ever insurgent let me be,
    Make me more daring than devout;
From sleek contentment keep me free,
    And fill me with a buoyant doubt.

Open my eyes to visions girt
    With beauty, and with wonder lit—
But let me always see the dirt,
    And all that spawn and die in it.

Open my eyes to music; let
    Me thrill with Spring's first flutes and drums—
But never let me dare forget
    The bitter ballads of the slums.

From compromise and things half-done,
    Keep me, with stern and stubborn pride.
And when, at last, the fight is won,
    God, keep me still unsatisfied.

Louis Untermeyer (1885–1977) was a poet and editor of more than one hundred books and anthologies. He served as poetry consultant to the Library of Congress from 1961 to 1963.

prayer from the philippines

∽— IONA COMMUNITY —∾

Lord, in these times,
when we fear we are losing hope
or feel that our efforts are futile,
let us see in our hearts and minds
the image of your resurrection,
and let that be our source of courage and strength.
With that, and in your company,
help us to face challenges and struggles
against all that is born of injustice.

This prayer from the Philippines is used by the Iona
Community in their worship. Members of the Iona Community,
based on the Scottish island of Iona, also live in various urban
centers around the world where they seek to live their common
life in the midst of violence.

CHAPTER 5

PRAYERS FOR TEACHING
AND DISCOVERING

"The school of today is the world of tomorrow," writes W. E. B. Du Bois in the first prayer of this chapter. How we come to view the world and our place in it is often most profoundly shaped by our schooling and by those teachers who have worked with us—pointing us in new directions, opening our eyes to a particular discipline, enabling our discovery.

These prayers help us to understand the great work of education as a partnership between those who teach and those who learn. They also help us to see God as collaborating with us in all our learning.

Some of these prayers are intended especially for teachers. "As I prepare for teaching," prays Sarah Klos, "make me first a learner." Gabriela Mistral, humbly aware that Christ was himself a teacher, asks that she "not be pained by the lack of understanding nor saddened by the forgetfulness" of those whom she has taught. And teacher J. M. Cameron asks God's help to induce the "right perplexities" in his students.

But just as a good teacher does not merely dispense knowledge, so, too, God participates with us, collaborating in all human disciplines. "You take the pen—and the lines dance," praises Dag Hammarskjöld. "You take the flute—and the notes shimmer." Poet E. E. Cummings wonders how any human can "doubt unimaginably You" and celebrates the senses of tasting, touching, hearing, and seeing. Scholar Jean-Pierre de Caussade sees God speaking through historical events, while Christina Rossetti prays for eyes to see the natural world so that "taught by such, we see / beyond all creatures thee." In this spirit, then, Walter Rauschenbusch prays that God will grant to teachers "an abiding consciousness that they are coworkers with you, great teacher of humanity."

"School" equips us for the larger "world," not only through the particular discipline we may have mastered, but also through the daily habits and the patterns we acquire in our course of study. Christina Rossetti asks for the grace "to teach in a teachable spirit; learning along with those we teach." Mary Stewart prays to be kept from pettiness: "Let us be large in thought." Even the cycle of academic life ("another class, another school year"), which prompts the prayer of Clifford Swartz, can remind us that every new course of study provides us with a fresh start. This, in itself, is a lesson in grace.

While prayers in previous chapters praise the source of all wisdom, seek God's guidance and direction, or ask for help in facing new challenges, all the prayers in this chapter express in various ways the simple request of Brother Lawrence: "Lord, work with me."

for the great work of education

∞— W. E. B. DU BOIS —∞

God bless all schools and forward the great work of education for which we stand. Arouse within us and within our land a deep realization of the seriousness of our problem of training children. On them rests the future work and thought and sentiment and goodness of the world. If here and elsewhere we train the lazy and shallow, the self-indulgent and the frivolous—if we destroy reason and religion and do not rebuild, help us, O God, to realize how heavy is our responsibility and how great the cost. The school of today is the world of tomorrow and today and tomorrow are Thine, O God. Amen.

One of the leading intellectuals of the early twentieth century, W. E. B. Du Bois (1868–1963) served on the board of the NAACP in its formative years. In his influential work *The Souls of Black Folk*, Du Bois wrote: "The function of the university is not simply to teach bread-winning, or to furnish teachers for the public schools or to be a centre of polite society; it is, above all, to be the organ of that fine adjustment between real life and the growing knowledge of life, an adjustment which forms the secret of civilization."

as i prepare for teaching

~ SARAH KLOS ~

As I prepare for teaching, O God,
Make me first a learner.
Only in this way can I stand in awe
Before your greatness
And, in some small way,
Teach others out of the fullness
Of my own devotion. Amen.

As a director of Christian education for more than twenty-five years, Sarah Klos developed a particular interest in global missions, serving on the board of the division for world missions and ecumenism with the Evangelical Lutheran Church in America.

to know that
which is worth knowing

∾ THOMAS À KEMPIS ∾

Grant, O Lord, to all students, to love that which is worth loving, to know that which is worth knowing, to praise that which pleaseth thee most, to esteem that which is most precious unto thee, and to dislike whatsoever is evil in thine eyes. Grant that with true judgment they may distinguish things that differ, and, above all, may search out and do what is well-pleasing unto thee; through Jesus Christ our Lord.

Born near Cologne, Germany, Thomas à Kempis (c.1380–1471) entered into a ministry in Holland at about age twenty. There he eventually became the superior while devoting himself to prayer, writing, copying, preaching, teaching, and reading. He lived to be over ninety years old. Originally written in Latin, Thomas à Kempis's *Imitation of Christ* is still considered a foremost work of Christian devotion and personal piety.

lord, grant us eyes to see

∽ CHRISTINA ROSSETTI ∽

Lord, grant us eyes to see
Within the seed a tree,
Within the glowing egg a bird,
Within the shroud a butterfly:
Till taught by such, we see
Beyond all creatures thee,
And hearken for thy tender word
And hear it, "Fear not: it is I."

Christina Rossetti (1830–94), a poet associated with the Pre-Raphaelite movement in England, was a devout Anglican whose life was dedicated to the care of her relatives and to charity. Although troubled by bouts of ill health, she published several collections of poetry in her lifetime, including *Goblin Market* and *The Prince's Progress.*

you take the pen

∾— DAG HAMMARSKJÖLD —∾

You take the pen—and the lines dance.
You take the flute—and the notes shimmer.
You take the brush—and the colors sing.
So all things have meaning and beauty in that space
    beyond time where You are.
How, then, can I hold back anything from You?

Dag Hammarskjöld (1905–61) served as the secretary-general of the United Nations from 1953 until 1961. The son of a Swedish prime minister, he studied law and economics at the universities of Uppsala and Stockholm. In his posthumously published book *Markings* he wrote, "Prayer, crystallized in words, assigns a permanent wave length on which the dialogue has to be continued, even when our mind is occupied with other matters."

the teacher

⌐ LESLIE PINCKNEY HILL ⌐

Lord, who am I to teach the way
To little children day by day.
So prone myself to go astray?

I teach them knowledge, but I know
How faint they flicker and how low
The candles of my knowledge glow.

I teach them power to will and do,
But only now to learn anew
My own great weakness thru and thru.

I teach them love for all mankind
And all God's creatures, but I find
My love comes lagging far behind.

Lord, if their guide I still must be.
Oh, let the little children see
The teacher leaning hard on Thee.

Known as both a teacher and a poet, Leslie Pinckney Hill (1880–1960) devoted his writing and career to promoting high standards in education as well as emphasizing African American contributions to America. After earning his B.A. and M.A. from Harvard, Hill contributed poems to collections such as *The Poetry of the Negro* and published a book of his own poems, *The Wings of Oppression*.

a prayer for the teacher

~ J. M. CAMERON ~

Lord God:
you who are present in all your creatures
and enable them to praise you,
help us to find your image in those we teach
and to ask them useful questions
and induce in them the right perplexities.

J. M. Cameron (1910–98) was educated at Oxford and lec-
tured at a number of universities in the United Kingdom,
Australia, and Canada. He wrote a number of books, including
*The Arts, Artists and Thinkers, Problems in Psychotherapy and
Jurisprudence,* and *John Henry Newman.*

for those estranged from you

∽ JOHANN HEERMANN ∽

O Christ our Light, O radiance true,
Shine forth on those estranged from you,
And bring them to your home again
Where their delight shall never end.

Fill with the radiance of your grace
The wanderer lost in error's maze.
Enlighten those whose secret minds
Some deep delusion haunts and blinds.

Lord, open all reluctant ears
And take away the childish fears
Of those who tremble to express
The faith their secret hearts confess.

Lord, let your mercy's gentle ray
Shine down on others strayed away.
To those in conscience wounded sore,
Show heaven's waiting, open door.

Born near Wohlau in present-day Poland, Johann Heermann (1585–1647) was the fifth and only surviving child whose mother vowed to educate him for the ministry if he survived. He served as pastor in the small town of Köben from 1611 to 1634. Heermann endured poor health throughout his life and, in his later years, the ravages of the Thirty Years War. Yet out of adversity he composed many enduring hymns.

the teacher's prayer

⌒ GABRIELA MISTRAL ⌒

Lord, you who taught, forgive me that I teach; forgive me that I bear the name of teacher, the name you bore on earth.

Grant me such devoted love for my school that not even beauty's flame will detract from my faithful tenderness.

Master, make my fervor long-lasting and my disillusion brief. Uproot from me this impure desire for justice that still troubles me, the petty protest that rises up within me when I am hurt. Let not the incomprehension of others trouble me, or the forgetfulness of those I have taught sadden me.

Let me be more maternal than a mother; able to love and defend with all of a mother's fervor the child that is not flesh of my flesh. Grant that I may be successful in molding one of my pupils into a perfect poem, and let me leave within her my deepest-felt melody that she may sing for you when my lips shall sing no more.

Make me strong in my faith that your Gospel is possible in my time, so that I do not renounce the daily battle to make it live.

A native of Chile, Gabriela Mistral (1889–1957) dedicated herself to education and diplomacy, working with the United Nations and teaching at Barnard, Vassar, and Middlebury. She received the 1945 Nobel Prize for literature.

a prayer for teachers

ᕽ— WALTER RAUSCHENBUSCH —ᕽ

We implore thy blessing, O God, on all the men and women who teach the children and youth of our nation, for they are the potent friends and helpers of our homes. Into their hands we daily commit the dearest that we have, and as they make our children, so shall future years see them. Grant them an abiding consciousness that they are coworkers with you, great teacher of humanity, and that you have charged them with the holy duty of bringing forth from the budding life of the young the mysterious stores of character and ability which you have hidden in them.

A Baptist minister, theologian, and educator, Walter Rauschenbusch (1861–1918) urged Christians to ally themselves with the working class and to seek social reform. His major work, *A Theology for the Social Gospel,* helped to shape the social gospel movement of the early twentieth century.

another class, another school year

᠀— CLIFFORD SWARTZ —᠀

Another class, another school year, Lord.
Tomorrow I must set the tone
For attention to mechanical
Procedures such as grading curves.
They'll listen carefully to that!
These crass details are part of teaching.
As with any trade, we must establish
Rules and then know how to break them.

Bur first, I think I'll ask these students
Where we are. It's easy to forget.
At times the world seems little larger
Than our campus, and for the young
It sometimes shrinks until there's barely
Room enough for one—or if they're lucky, two.
The world is wide in many ways.
In every course we should take journeys
To the boundaries of our knowledge.
The teacher's role in this is not
To specify and plot old routes.
These, the students find embedded
In their texts, complete with diagrams.

Instead, we serve as guides, who have gone down
These roads before, but have not taken
All the side paths, and have not reached the end.

We must be sure our students know
That there are roads we have not taken.
We must prepare them to abandon us
And forge ahead when we turn back.
All we can do is choose the early paths
And with delight cry out, "Oh, look!"
At sights along the way.

Another year, another journey, Lord.
I hope that on a distribution curve
Of distance gone and paths explored
My students all may earn high grades.
But failing that, I pray that I can use such skill
In crying "Look, oh, look!" that each, if only once,
May answer with excitement, "Yes, I see, I see!"

Besides writing prayers, Clifford Swartz has written two books on physics: *A Search for Order in the Physical Universe* and *Prelude to Physics*. He is the editor of *The Physics Teacher*.

in time of examination

⁓ KATHARINE LEE ⁓

O God, who didst give Thy Holy Spirit to guide and strengthen Thy people, fill us now with this same spirit that we may approach the coming examinations with a quiet mind. May the flame of Thy Spirit illumine our thinking and strengthen us to rise above any temptation that may beset us. Grant us a good memory and a wise understanding of what we have learned. May all that we undertake be done to the best of the ability which Thou gavest us. This we ask in the name of Thy dear Son, who Himself was a teacher, Jesus Christ, Our Lord.

Katharine Lee was principal of the National Cathedral School for girls from 1950 to 1968. Born to outstanding parents (her father was a general in the United States Army and her mother helped to organize the nurse's branch of the army after the Spanish-American War), Lee herself received her B.A. from Mount Holyoke and her M.A. from Columbia University. After teaching at several schools in the United States and England, she came to the Cathedral School, where she was especially known for her chapel talks and Bible classes.

rekindle our sense of wonder

 JOHN MALCUS ELLISON

Thou, who art the eternal God and our Father, hast set before each of us an untraveled way full of beauty and mystery, and calling for courage and the spirit of adventure. Grant us Thy kindly light to lead us onward. To the youth of this day in all nations, give us a vision of Thy purpose for their lives; and to us who are older, grant a return of the wonder which was the glory of our youth and which as we beheld it brought Thy light into our hearts. Oh, let not the wonder fade or the light become darkness, lest we lose our way. In His Name. Amen.

John Malcus Ellison (1889–1979) served as a preacher, a high school principal, and a professor at Howard and Virginia Union universities. He was the first African American to become president (and later, chancellor) of Virginia Union University. Dr. Ellison was the author of *Tensions and Destiny* (1953), *They Who Preach* (1956), and *They Sang through the Crisis: Dealing with Life's Most Critical Issues* (1961).

teach me, lord, to read the book of life

⌁— JEAN-PIERRE DE CAUSSADE —⌁

You speak, Lord, to all men in general through general events. Revolutions are simply the tides of your Providence, which stir up storms and tempests in people's minds. You speak to men in particular through particular events, as they occur moment by moment. But instead of hearing your voice, instead of respecting events as signals of your loving guidance, people see nothing else but blind chance and human decision. They find objections to everything you say. They wish to add to or subtract from your Word. They wish to change and reform it.

Teach me, dear Lord, to read clearly this book of life. I wish to be like a simple child, accepting your word regardless of whether I understand your purposes. It is enough for me that you speak.

As a Jesuit priest in France, Jean-Pierre de Caussade (1675–1751) taught that God is present in all events and that we should submit to God's will. Two centuries after his death, his reflections were published under the title *Self-Abandonment to Divine Providence*, a book that has become a spiritual classic.

i thank you, god

～ E. E. CUMMINGS ～

i thank You God for most this amazing
day:for the leaping greenly spirits of trees
and a blue true dream of sky; and for everything
which is natural which is infinite which is yes

(i who have died am alive again today,
and this is the sun's birthday;this is the birth
day of life and of love and wings:and of the gay
great happening illimitably earth)

how should tasting touching hearing seeing
breathing any—lifted from the no
of all nothing—human merely being
doubt unimaginably You?

(now the ears of my ears awake and
now the eyes of my eyes are opened)

When Edward Estlin Cummings (1894–1962) was born in
Cambridge, Massachusetts, his father was teaching in the English
department at Harvard. Later his father became the pastor of the
famous Old South Church in Boston. E. E. Cummings received
his B.A. and M.A. from Harvard and then served in an ambulance
corps in World War I. His poems continue to delight readers with
their experiments in punctuation, phrasing, and stream-of-con-
sciousness techniques.

praise the lord

∽ ERNESTO CARDENAL ∾

Praise the Lord in his cosmos
Praise him in his sanctuary
Praise him with a radio-signal
    100,000 million light-years away
Praise him in the stars
               in inter-stellar space
Praise him in the galaxies
                       in inter-galactic space
Praise him in atoms
               in inter-atomic space
Praise him on violin and flute
                  on the saxophone
Praise him with clarinet and horn
    with cornet and trombone
        on alto-sax and trumpet
Praise him with viola and cello
        on piano and harpsichord
Praise him with blues and jazz
                  with an orchestra
Praise him with spirituals
        with soul-music and Beethoven's fifth
        with marimbas and guitars

Praise him with discs and cassettes
        with high-fi systems
        and quadraphonic sound
Let everything that draws breath praise him
        Alleluia!
Let all living cells praise the Lord
        Alleluia!
                Praise the Lord!

Born in Nicaragua, Ernesto Cardenal is an internationally known poet who is also recognized as a strong voice for social justice. Cardenal was educated at the University of Mexico and Columbia University. After his conversion to Christianity, he studied with the Trappist monk Thomas Merton at Gethsemani, Kentucky, and in 1965 he was ordained as a Roman Catholic priest. Back in his native Nicaragua, Cardenal developed a more radical understanding of Christianity, actively supporting the revolution against the dictator Somoza. After the revolution, Cardenal was appointed minister of culture. He continues to make his home in Nicaragua. This prayer of praise is based on Psalm 150.

prayer of learned yearning

∽ KATHERINE JUUL NEVINS ∼

The night before the last day of class—
A strange time to be reflecting on
wishes and hopes and dreams and prayers
for those who have spent every weekday morning
listening to names and dates,
remembering something, or maybe nothing
of consequence.
    Yet, it is the stories that I want them to hear.
Others' stories that come alive,
so that they might become more intrigued with
    their own.

I wish for them

To draw wisdom from lessons in failure,
in lives worn down, worn thin, worn out;
and lessons of triumph from those who persevered,
    overcame,
adapted, adopted, transpired, transformed . . . changed.

I wish for them

To be thankful for the women who bore them,
for their matriarchal lineage that endured great pain
to further the gift of life.

To be thankful for the women who go before them:
ordinary women doing extraordinary things,
now extraordinary women doing ordinary things,
who carved a path for themselves in treacherous
    terrains
that we might later come to stroll more freely among
    the hills and plains.

To be thankful for who they are and will become:
more centered, more holy,
never sure, but more secure
in the discovery of themselves,
the giving of gifts, the fulfillment of their calling.

God, nurture the inner light that they might shine
    in any darkness,
And let no human hinder their way.
May they know Joy.
May they know Love.
May they know Peace.
Amen.

Katherine Juul Nevins grew up in Kansas. She is professor of psychology at Bethel College in St. Paul, Minnesota, and focuses on women's concerns and development, conflict resolution, and organizational facilitation. She loves music, woodworking, and nature.

a prayer for teachers

ᔷ— CHRISTINA ROSSETTI —ᔷ

Lord Jesus, merciful and patient, grant us grace, I beseech thee, ever to teach in a teachable spirit; learning along with those we teach, and learning from them whenever thou so pleasest. Word of God, speak to us, speak by us, what thou wilt. Wisdom of God, instruct us, instruct by us, if and whom thou wilt. Eternal Truth, reveal thyself to us, reveal thyself by us, in whatsoever measure thou wilt; that we and they may all be taught of God.

For a brief time in her twenties, Christina Rossetti (1830–94) taught a day school with her mother to support the family. She was a devout, evangelical Anglican who dedicated her life to the care of her relatives and to charity. Although troubled by bouts of ill health, she published several collections of poetry that are still studied today.

keep us, oh god, from pettiness

᠀— MARY STEWART —᠀

Keep us, Oh God, from pettiness; let us be large in
    thought, in word, in deed.
Let us be done with fault-finding and leave off
    self-seeking.
May we put away all pretense and meet each other face
    to face—without self-pity and without prejudice.
May we never be hasty in judgment and always
    generous.
Let us take time for all things; make us to grow calm,
    serene, gentle.
Teach us to put into action our better impulses,
    straightforward and unafraid.
Grant that we may realize that it is the little things
    that create differences, that in the big things of
    life we are at one.
And may we strive to touch and to know the great,
    common heart of us all, and, Oh Lord God,
    let us forget not to be kind!

A scholar of classical literature, Mary Stewart (1878–1943)
served as superintendent of education for the Indians of
California. She campaigned vigorously for the causes of women.

lord, work with me

↶ BROTHER LAWRENCE ↷

My God, since You are with me, and since it is Your will that I should apply my mind to these outward things, I pray that You will give me the grace to remain with You and keep company with You.

But so that my work may be better, Lord, work with me; receive my work and possess all my affections. Amen.

Born in France, Brother Lawrence (1611–91) had no formal education and served as a soldier and servant. In 1666 he became a lay brother in the Carmelite Order in Paris, where he worked in the kitchen until eighty years of age. His life modeled a blending of work and prayer. This prayer is from his famous book, *Practicing the Presence of God.*

CHAPTER 6

PRAYERS FOR THE WORLD AS LOVE WOULD MAKE

Deeper wisdom and understanding—with their joys come responsibilities and stresses. Complacency and superiority lure us; we are tempted to settle down, put our feet up, and ponder all we have learned. Sometimes we wish that the privilege of learning didn't have fine print at the bottom, calling us to look in new directions.

Wisdom calls us, compelling us to look within. People we think of as wise have the quality of seeing themselves clearly. They don't fly off in different directions, but they wait for the vision to act. And perhaps most important, they act out of a clear sense of being loved.

But the gaze inside becomes a look outside as we turn to look deeply at the world. Wisdom compels us to try to see the world from God's perspective. We look beyond ourselves for a vision of a "world as love would make." Deeper understanding brings us deeper compassion. We ask with Walter Rauschenbusch, "Though increase of knowledge bring increase of sorrow, may we . . . offer ourselves as instruments of your spirit in bringing order and beauty out of disorder and darkness." This vision can be painful.

And the vision can be challenging. The prayers in this chapter are requests, not only for understanding and vision, but also for the wisdom to use our newfound knowledge. Finding ways to move forward may be the most demanding work we ever do. Our lives may be unsettled. We pray for the courage to create, following in the path of our Creator God; we pray for the will to work; we pray to be useful to God.

These are prayers of courage rather than comfort, of challenge rather than solace. Our learning, soaked with much prayer, leads to wisdom, and our wisdom to vision, "till our goals and [God's] are one." This is the life of risking faith that St. Augustine prays about, in which we find ourselves walking with the God, "whom to serve is perfect freedom."

prayers for guidance

∽ AUGUSTINE ∼

O Thou, from whom to be turned is to fall,
    to whom to be turned is to rise,
    and in whom to stand is to abide for ever:
Grant us in all our duties thy help,
    in all our perplexities thy guidance,
    in all our dangers thy protection,
    and in all our sorrows thy peace;
through Jesus Christ our Lord.

Eternal God, who are the light of the minds that
    know thee,
    the joy of the hearts that love thee,
    and the strength of the wills that serve thee:
Grant us so to know thee that we may truly love thee,
    and so to love thee that we may fully serve thee,
    whom to serve is perfect freedom,
in Jesus Christ our Lord.

Augustine (354–430) is generally regarded as the father of
the Western church. Born in what is now Algeria, he became
a skilled rhetorician and eventually experienced a wonderful
conversion while reading Romans 13 in a garden. By 396 he
had become a bishop. Living and writing during the collapse of
the Roman Empire, he developed doctrines of original sin,
predestination, and grace that were to shape the teachings of the
medieval church.

help us to do our daily work

꩜— JOHN R. W. STOTT —꩜

Heavenly Father, you have blessed our weekday work both by your own work of creation and by your Son's labour at a carpenter's bench: give the nation's leaders the wisdom to solve the problem of unemployment. Enable those of us with work to do, not only to find fulfillment in it ourselves, but also to enjoy the privilege of cooperating with you in the service of the community, through Jesus Christ our Lord.

꩜ Educated at Cambridge, John R. W. Stott was ordained in the Anglican Church in 1945. A leader in the Anglican evangelical movement, he is well known as the author of many books, ranging from theological commentaries on the New Testament, such as *The Message of Galatians* and *The Message of Thessalonians*, to his evangelistic book *Basic Christianity*, to the major study called *The Cross of Christ.* Stott directs the London Institute for Contemporary Christianity and is an avid bird-watcher.

for integrity

◇— ROBERT A. RAINES —◇

O God, make me discontent with things the way
they are in the world,
   and in my own life.
Teach me how to blush again,
   for the tawdry deals,
       the arrogant-but-courteous prejudice,
       the snickers,
       the leers,
       the good food and drink which make me
           too weary to repent.
       the flattery given and received,
       my willing use of rights and privileges
           other men are unfairly denied.
Make me notice the stains when people get spilled on.
Make me care about the slum child downtown,
       the misfit at work,
       the people crammed into the mental hospital,
       the men, women, and youth behind bars.
Jar my complacence; expose my excuses; get me
   involved
   in the life of my city,
   and give me integrity once more.

Robert A. Raines was educated at Yale and Cambridge before being ordained as a Methodist minister in 1953. Raines is the author of *Reshaping the Christian Life*, *Creative Brooding*, and *A Time to Live*.

spirit of integrity

∽ JANET MORLEY ∽

Spirit of integrity,
you drive us into the desert
to search out our truth.
Give us clarity to know what is right,
and courage to reject what is strategic;
that we may abandon the false innocence
of failing to choose at all,
but may follow the purposes of Jesus Christ.
Amen.

Activist, writer, and editor, Janet Morley works as adult education adviser for Christian Aid, a relief organization. Her collections include *Celebrating Women* and *Bread of Tomorrow: Praying with the World's Poor.*

prayer for vision

∽ W. E. B. DU BOIS ∽

Grant us, O God, the vision and the will to be found on the right side in the great battle for bread, which rages round us, in strike and turmoil and litigation. Let us remember that here as so often elsewhere no impossible wisdom is asked of men, only Thine ancient sacrifice—to do justly and love mercy and walk humbly—to refuse to use, of the world's goods, more than we earn, to be generous with those that earn but little and to avoid the vulgarity that flaunts wealth and clothes and ribbons in the face of poverty. These things are the sins that lie beneath our labor wars, and from such sins defend us, O Lord. Amen.

As an undergraduate at Fisk University, W. E. B. Du Bois (1868–1963) spent his summers teaching at rural schools in Tennessee and was deeply moved by the effects of the chronic racial oppression he witnessed. Years later, as a professor of economics and sociology at Atlanta University (1897–1910), he wrote this prayer, among many others, for his students.

the way of the cross

✎— CARYLL HOUSELANDER —✎

Grant to us, Lord,
that the shock of the first sin,
of the first failure
at the beginning of life,
may give us self-knowledge
and a truer knowledge of You;
may help us to know ourselves
and You,
and to know the depths of Your love.
May it teach us
our dependence on You,
and that without You
we can do nothing.

Turn the humiliation
caused by our vanity
into Your humility,
and lift us up in Your power
and with Your courage
to take the cross
and to start again on the way,
trusting now,
not in ourselves
but in You.

Associated with an advertising firm in London, Caryll
Houselander (1901–54) also wrote *The Way of the Cross* and *The
Comforting of Christ.*

thank you for unsettling our lives

∾ STANLEY HAUERWAS ∾

Almighty God, whose Mary-like beauty compels our attention, give us hearts that jump within us with the good news of your salvation. We confess that amidst the tedium of the everyday our worship of you sometimes feels like a job—just "one more thing." Thank you for the unsettling of our lives, wherein we discover the splendor of the kingdom made possible by your Son, Jesus Christ. We pray that you will ever be here, unsettling our attempts to domesticate the wildness of your Spirit. Amen.

"The church does not have a social ethic," Professor Stanley Hauerwas once said; "the church is a social ethic." Professor Hauerwas teaches theological ethics at the Divinity School, Duke University. He is the author of many influential books, including *A Community of Character: Toward a Constructive Christian Social Ethic* (1981) and *In Good Company: The Church as Polis* (1995). He is highly respected for his commitment to Christian faith and for his "unsettling" ideas about the role of the church in the world.

be thou my vision

~ TRADITIONAL GAELIC HYMN ~

Be thou my vision, O Lord of my heart;
Naught be all else to me, save that thou art.
Thou my best thought, by day or night,
Waking or sleeping, thy presence my light.

Be thou my wisdom, and thou my true word;
I ever with thee and thou with me, Lord;
Thou and thou only, first in my heart,
Great God of heaven, my treasure thou art.

Great God of heaven, my victory won,
May I reach heaven's joys, O bright heaven's Sun!
Heart of my own heart, whatever befall,
Still be my vision, O Ruler of all.

This beloved hymn is of Irish origin and dates from around
700. It was translated by Mary Elizabeth Byrne (1880–1931) and
versified by Eleanor H. Hull (1860–1935).

come to us, creative spirit

⌐ FRANCIS POTT ⌐

Come to us, creative Spirit.
In our Father's house;
every human talent hallow,
hidden skills arouse,
that within your earthly temple,
wise and simple
may rejoice.

Poet, painter, music-maker
all your treasures bring,
craftsman, actor, graceful dancer
make your offering,
join your hands in celebration;
let creation
shout and sing!

Word from God eternal springing
fill our minds, we pray;
and in all artistic vision
give integrity:
may the flame within us burning
kindle yearning
day by day.

Educated at Oxford, Francis Pott (1832–1909) was pastor of a number of churches. He is best remembered for the hymns "Angel Voices Ever Singing" and "The Strife Is O'er, the Battle Done."

give us, o god,
a vision of your world

⌀ WOMEN'S WORLD ⌀
DAY OF PRAYER

Give us, O God, a vision of your world as love
    would make it;
a world where the weak are protected and none
    go hungry;
a world whose benefits are shared, so that everyone
    can enjoy them;
a world whose different people and cultures live
    with tolerance and mutual respect;
a world where peace is built with justice,
and justice is fired with love;
Lord Jesus Christ, give us the courage to build.

Since 1919, the Women's World Day of Prayer has become an international ecumenical movement of Christian women, observed on the first Friday in March of each year. This anonymous prayer was used for the 1993 Women's World Day of Prayer. It is included in Kathy Keay's collection *Laughter, Silence, and Shouting: An Anthology of Women's Prayers*.

a prayer for zeal

⌒ EDWARD HAYS ⌒

Implant within my heart, O God,
    the fiery zeal of a Jeremiah,
    the conviction of a Ruth or Rebecca
    and the zest of a Francis of Assisi.

Stir my slumbering soul,
    that it might sing a song of passion and devotion,
    drunk with dancing joy and desire for you,
    my divine and loving Friend.

May my heart be as hot as the heart of Moses
    for all your children burdened by slavery,
    for all who feel oppression's steely heel
    or suffer rejection in an alien land.

May I, like your son Jesus,
    be consumed with zeal for you, Divine Beloved,
    for life, for justice and for peace;
    for all that I know in faith.

Fill me with zeal, O God.

Edward Hays is a Roman Catholic priest who believes that
"prayers for justice and peace for all who dwell on this planet
must be an essential part of our practice." This prayer appears in
his collection *Prayers for a Planetary Pilgrim*, a work that has
appealed to people from various religious traditions.

a prayer for those without knowledge

∽— WALTER RAUSCHENBUSCH —∾

We pray for those who amid all the knowledge of our day are still without knowledge; for those who hear not the sighs of the children that toil, nor the sobs of such as are wounded because others have made haste to be rich; for those who have never felt the hot tears of the mothers of the poor that struggle vainly against poverty and vice. Arouse them, we beseech you, from their selfish comfort and grant them the grace of social repentance. Smite us all with the conviction that for us ignorance is sin, and that we are indeed our brother's keeper if our own hand has helped to lay him low. Though increase of knowledge bring increase of sorrow, may we turn without flinching to the light and offer ourselves as instruments of your spirit in bringing order and beauty out of disorder and darkness.

A Baptist minister, theologian, and educator, Walter Rauschenbusch (1861–1918) urged Christians to ally themselves with the working class and to seek social reform. His books, including *Christianizing the Social Order* and *A Theology for the Social Gospel*, were formative to many Christians in the early twentieth century.

send us out

∽ SHEILA CASSIDY ∼

Lord of the Universe
look in love upon your people.
Pour the healing oil of your compassion
on a world that is wounded and dying.
Send us out in search of the lost,
to comfort the afflicted,
to bind up the broken,
and to free those trapped
under the rubble of their fallen dreams.

Born in Australia, Sheila Cassidy went to medical school in England. In 1975, while practicing medicine in Chile, she was arrested and tortured for treating a revolutionary. For more than a decade, she served as medical director of St. Luke's Hospice in Plymouth, England. In 1996 Dr. Cassidy founded Jeremiah's Journey, a program for helping bereaved children. She is the author of *Audacity to Believe* and *Sharing the Darkness: The Spirituality of Caring.*

teach me the dignity of labor

∾ F. B. MEYER ∾

Almighty God, teach me the dignity of labor, the honor of industrious toil, the glory of being able to do something in the world. Forgive, I pray thee, my shortcomings and failure, prosper and establish the work of my hands. Make my life deeper, stronger, richer, gentler, more Christlike, more full of the spirit of Heaven, more devoted to thy service and glory. Amen.

Born in London and ordained as a Baptist minister, F. B. Meyer (1847–1929) was a Bible expositor and the author of some forty books. He preached widely throughout the world.

for renewal

᠊ GEORGE APPLETON ᠊

O my God,
grant that I may so wait upon thee,
that when quick decision and action are needed
I may mount up with wings as an eagle;
and when under direction of thy will
and the needs of people
I have to keep going under pressure,
I may run and not be weary;
and in times of routine and humble duty,
I may walk and not faint.
For all my fresh springs are in thee,
O God of my strength.

Born in 1902, George Appleton became an Anglican priest and served in England, Burma, India, and Australia. In 1968 he was appointed Anglican archbishop in Jerusalem, where he served until 1974, seeking to build bridges between the Christian, Jewish, and Muslim communities. George Appleton edited *The Oxford Book of Prayer.*

govern all by thy wisdom

∽— TERESA OF ÁVILA —∽

Govern all by thy wisdom, O Lord, so that my soul may be serving thee as thou dost will, and not as I may choose. Do not punish me, I beseech thee, by granting that which I wish or ask, if it offend thy love, which would always live in me. Let me die to myself, that I may serve thee, who in thyself art the true life. Amen.

Descended from an old Spanish family, Teresa of Ávila (1515–82) entered a Carmelite monastery at age twenty. Throughout her life she established houses of prayer and wrote of her deepening spiritual experiences and instructions for cultivating the life of prayer.

burdens

ᕐ JOHN CALVIN REID ᕐ

I would remember, O God, that there are some burdens I am called upon to carry—the burden of responsibility, the burden of honest labor, the burden of duty, the burden of sympathetic concern for the needs of others. I pray not for relief from these burdens, but for strength to bear them with courage and cheerfulness.

But I would remember also that I am not called to carry the burden of guilt, of fear, of anxiety. I pray for relief from these, that my shoulders may be free and strong to carry the burdens I should bear.

Above all, so fill my heart with the spirit of Christ that I shall find his yoke easy and his burden light. Amen.

Born in South Carolina and educated in Pittsburgh, Edinburgh, and Oxford, John Calvin Reid pastored a number of Presbyterian churches during his ministry. His many books include *Parables from Nature*, *Secrets from Field and Forest*, and *Thirty Favorite Bible Stories*.

still let thy wisdom be my guide

ᐁ— JOHN WESLEY —ᐃ

Still let thy wisdom be my guide,
Nor take thy flight from me away;
Still with me let thy grace abide,
That I from thee may never stray:
Let thy word richly in me dwell,
Thy peace and love my portion be;
My joy to endure and do thy will,
Till perfect I am found in thee. Amen.

Fifteenth child of Samuel and Susanna Wesley, John Wesley (1703–91) was educated at Oxford and traveled with his brother Charles on a ministry trip to Georgia. He had a conversion experience in 1738 and became a well-known preacher and the leader of the Methodist movement.

for writers and for readers

~ CHARLES KINGSLEY ~

O Thou Teacher of all truth, Christ our Lord, raise up, we beseech thee, in this our day wise and holy writers, and grant them words and utterance to speak to all hearts the message of thy covenant; and to us give grace to take care what we read and how we read, and above all to hold us fast by the Book of books, and by thee, the very Word of God, for ever and ever.

Charles Kingsley (1819–75), English clergyman and professor of modern history at Cambridge University, was influenced at an early age by his reading of *The Kingdom of Christ* (1838) by Frederick Denison Maurice (1805–72), who argued that Christians should be involved in social issues. As a writer, Kingsley sought to expose social injustice among working people in such historical novels as *Alton Locke* (1850), *Hypatia* (1853), and *The Water Babies* (1863), his best-known work.

to serve you in the public worlds

ᴗ— IONA COMMUNITY —ᴗ

Liberate all who follow Christ
from narrowness of vision
and limited discipleship.
Make your people keen to serve you
in the public worlds of business,
politics, education, law, industry
and wherever the welfare of humanity
may be improved or threatened.
Thus may compassion and justice
inform our national life and institutions
as keenly as they address our consciences.
Amen.

In the years of the Great Depression, the Reverend George
MacLeod took a group of trainee ministers and unemployed ship-
builders to the island of Iona off the coast of Scotland. There,
where pilgrims have been drawn for centuries, they established an
ecumenical Christian community, committed to a life of discipline, accountability, and labor for peace and justice. Members of
the Iona Community today serve Christ in the public world as
well as on the island.

make me willing to be used by you

∽ ALAN PATON ∽

Lord, make me willing to be used by you. May my knowledge of my unworthiness never make me resist being used by you. May the need of others always be remembered by me, so that I may ever be willing to be used by you.

And open my eyes and my heart that I may this coming day be able to do some work of peace for you.

Political and social activist, educator, and writer, Alan Paton (1903–88) was born in Natal, South Africa. He taught school and was principal of a reformatory for a number of years. He is best known for his novels *Cry the Beloved Country* (1948) and *Too Late the Phalarope* (1953). Paton also wrote a number of nonfiction works on suffering and South Africa.

benediction

∾ TERESA OF ÁVILA ∾

Christ has no body now on earth but yours;
yours are the only hands with which he can do his
    work,
yours are the only feet with which he can go about
    the world,
yours are the only eyes through which his compassion
can shine forth upon a troubled world.
Christ has no body on earth now but yours.

Teresa of Ávila (1515–82) is best known as a person who
combined a deep prayer life with ceaseless activity as an organiz-
er and reformer, showing that the life of prayer can be a dynamic
force for action in the world.

ᧁ AUTHOR INDEX ᧁ